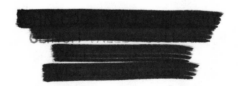

Reading Problems
Identification and Treatment

Reading Problems
Identification and Treatment

Peter Edwards

with additional material by Bridie Raban

HEINEMANN

Heinemann Educational Books Ltd
Halley Court, Jordan Hill, Oxford OX2 8EJ
OXFORD LONDON EDINBURGH MELBOURNE
SYDNEY AUCKLAND IBADAN NAIROBI
GABARONE HARARE KINGSTON
PORTSMOUTH NH (USA) SINGAPORE MADRID

ISBN 0 435 10264 8

Printed in Great Britain by
J. W. Arrowsmith Ltd, Bristol

Contents

Introduction

This book is intended for educators, parents and others who are interested in helping children to overcome reading problems. It incorporates the latest research findings with established methods of treating reading disabilities and offers practical suggestions in an easy-to-follow format.

Reading Problems: Identification and Treatment, is designed to facilitate reader self-direction and is organized along the following lines:

Problem: Each of the six main chapters deals with a major type of reading difficulty experienced by many children. Each problem is treated under a series of subheadings: *Possible Causes, Signs of Disability, Remedial Work, Sample Exercises, Teaching Suggestions* (which list appropriate remedial methods suggested by leading educationalists), and *Instructional Materials* (either commercially available or teacher/pupil constructed).

There follows a case study involving a young reader who has many of the reading disabilities discussed in the book. The treatment procedure is outlined and the first detailed lesson plan (Appendix C) is offered as a model for future lessons.

Generally speaking, the book is best used by turning to the chapter which deals with the type of problem causing difficulty, and then working through the various sections until the best course of action is determined.

Not all of the ideas, materials, and teaching suggestions in the book originated with the writer. Much of the content has been derived from other writers and the work of a number of graduate students. The book is offered as a practical solution to the problem of assisting many of the reading disability cases in today's schools and clinics.

This book was first published in Australia and it has been extensively revised for UK publication. The sections in each chapter headed Instructional Materials (Commercial) were devised by Bridie Raban of the Bristol Reading Centre.

Problem 1 Insufficient Sight Vocabulary

1 Insufficient Sight Vocabulary

The child lacks the ability to group words into thought units which are necessary for comprehension and fluency. He is handicapped in attempting to identify new words by the use of context clues, because the vocabulary load of unknown words is too great.

Possible Causes

1 Lack of experiential background.
2 Lack of incentive.
3 Limited reading experience.
4 Over-use of alphabet and phonic methods in beginning instruction.
5 Small speaking vocabulary.

Signs of Disability

1 The child may be a word-by-word reader. To test this make a flash or quick exposure of common words. If the child makes a considerably greater number of errors when words are flashed than when looking at words for an unlimited time, he can be assumed to have an insufficient sight vocabulary.
2 He may make phonic errors with words which should be known by sight.
3 He may fail to phrase well in oral reading.
4 He has a tendency to make an equal number of errors regardless of the difficulty of the material being read.
5 He will have a tendency to make many mistakes on small words as well as polysyllabic words.

Remedial Work

1 This work is best done by using reading material at a level of difficulty appropriate to the child.
2 The exercises that require rapid reading to locate a specific statement or to understand the general significance of the passage should be emphasized.
3 All the exercises suggested in the manual which require the new vocabulary to be read as whole words should be used but all those which require the analysis of words should be avoided.
4 Extensive reading of material related to the topic in the material being used is desirable. Such material should be at a level of difficulty that is definitely easy for the child, so that rapid recognition of words is encouraged.
5 Flashing words may be used to a limited extent in giving practice in quick word recognition but it tends to encourage guessing because it is a drill device devoid of a meaningful setting.

Sample Exercises:

The following are exercises for overcoming specific difficulties. The vocabulary used in the exercises may be adjusted to the level of difficulty required by the particular pupil concerned.

1 Exercises in which the word is so much expected that the recognition will be rapid.

A cowboy rides a _____.

    tree   horse   farm

2 Exercises in which a child finds the correct word in a list on the blackboard as the teacher gives the clue.

Find the word in this list that tells us where we:

Clue	*Word*
buy food	farm
go swimming	table
find cows	shop
eat dinner	beach

3 Exercises which require meaningful scanning of a list.

a) See how fast you can draw a line around all the things that can run.

horse	house	girl	pig
tree	dog	road	man
cat	boy	shop	window

b) Children place sight words on cards into meaningful groups. (Classification activity.) e.g.

Sight vocabulary: jam, blue, red, tiger, kangaroo, bread, yellow, butter, kitten.

Groups: *Food   Colours   Animals*

4 Various word games that call for immediate responses and require sight recognition of words and their meanings.

a) Cards with verbs printed on them and the child tells which words on the cards tell movement.

b) Word games similar to 'Authors', 'Bingo', 'Dominoes'.

The child needs experience in recognizing the word and its meaning at a glance.

5 *'Yes'— 'No'*. Teacher holds a card with a word printed on it and asks the children questions about the word which require a simple 'yes' or 'no' answer. Children respond with 'yes' or 'no' orally, or hold up a *yes/no* card.

6 *1,2,3*. Teacher prints three words on a card and a number (1,2 or 3) under each word. The teacher then asks questions about the words and the children hold up a *1,2* or *3* card to indicate which word is being discussed.

7 *Function words*. Teach function words in the context of meaningful phrases and sentences. Teacher says, 'The dog is _____' and children (or teacher) hold up a flash card with a concluding phrase: e.g. '*in* the house', or '*in*

the yard'. It is important to use the same function word (e.g. .'*in*') for a series of drills. (See Appendix A for the 100 most frequent words of Appendix B for a list of 800 'easy' words)

Teaching Suggestions

The following suggestions are drawn from the work of reading specialists. Sources are listed under the authors' names in the bibliography.

Betts:

After appropriate readiness activities, use:

Context or meaning clues — the most important
a) supply a word that seems to fit the context;
b) examine the context for a clue to the meaning.

Activities:

1 Labels on everything
2 Bulletin boards
3 Guided questions, comments, suggestions
4 Key sentences on the board
5 Multiple-choice activities
6 Completion exercises
7 Matching parts of sentences
8 Predicting events
9 Match words to pictures

Picture clues

1 Telling a story from illustrations
2 Preparing titles for pictures
3 Labelling objects
4 Matching words and pictures
5 Matching story parts to illustrations
6 Picture dictionaries

Configuration clues

Activities:

1 Teacher explains visual characteristics of word
2 Matching title and context words
3 Matching same word in large and small type
4 Matching same word in group
5 Underline the word that teacher says
6 Matching by superimposing with transparent paper
7 Matching phrases

Bond and Tinker:

Use an easy reader.

Use all exercises suggested in the teachers' manual which require new vocabulary to read as whole words.

Use workbook pages that emphasize word recognition rather than analysis.

Extensive reading of material related to topic in reader being used.

Various games calling for immediate responses and sight recognition of words and their meanings.

Exercises that require: meaningful scanning of a list; rapid reading to locate a specific statement or to understand general significance of passage.

Drummond and Wignell:

Use the word in context — orally.
Use the word in context — printed.
Illustrate the meaning of the word.
Place the word on a flashcard.
Use matching exercises — picture/word.
Locate word in a picture dictionary.
Use multi-sensory activities — tracing, miming.
Use labels, directions, charts, etc.

Durrell:

Emphasize meaning of the word.
Children should be given special perceptual training.
Stress word meaning.
Use context clues.
Use flash cards after the word has been taught.

Drill for words using tachistoscope (quick exposure device).
Individual picture dictionaries.

Gilliland:

Use oral impress method (pupil is trained to read in unison with teacher).
Practise with 'common' vocabulary.
Read very easy material.
Play games like 'Word Bingo'.
Practise with flash cards.
Have pupils act out the words in groups.
Check to see if easy words are being missed while harder words are known. If so, test the easy words in isolation and if comprehension is good, don't remediate.
Practise with a tachistoscope.
Use word box (keep a record of errors for each pupil).
Give some kinaesthetic instruction.

Gillespie and Johnson:

Separate words in a sentence by using pieces of coloured material.
Use markers to isolate words and emphasize the word/background relationship.

Nicholson:

Experiential approach — teacher writes child's story into a booklet.
Look — say.
Kinaesthetic method — child traces large copy of a word.
Non-visual method — word is traced on a child's back.
Visual imagery — child memorizes word 'picture'.
Story method — repetition of basic words.
Visual clues — words and pictures.

Otto & McMenemy:

Teach words in context.
Use experience chart, flash cards.
Give drill exercise using frequently confused pairs of words in sentences which give context clues; e.g. (house and horse; will and well; flop and flip).

Wilson:
The sight vocabulary must be overlearned through repeated
use in various contexts.

Specific type error	Remediation	
	Classroom	Clinical
1) Mistake small similar words	Teach discrimination of minimally different words in context, e.g. programmed materials using forced choice closure. Experience charts.	Same as classroom plus linguistic approaches as well.
2) Missed words are abstract concepts (function words)	Emphasize word in context whether experience story or drill.	Same as classroom plus have child build sentence from word cards, then rearrange the word order and correct it to show contrast in sentence meaning.
3) Known word not recognized in context	Exercise sight words in context through experience stories, sentences from prepared material, or written by teacher. It is important to begin and end drill on word in context. Highlight the word. Cards are made of each child's use of word in sentence, then cards are exchanged and they read each other's cards.	
4) Pronounced but not understood	Begin and end drill in *context*. Present word in various settings. Group experience stories. Study synonyms and antonyms. Use of dictionary for older students. Enrich experiential background.	Use non-oral reading approach to minimize pronunciation. Child responds physically to written command using slides or picture word cards. Match a picture with a printed word. Build sentence from word cards.
5) Word pronounced after undue hesitation	Timed or flashed exposure. Flash cards, word in isolation, then context. Set strict time limits. Set short term goals.	*Tachistoscope, Flash X*, home-made slides. Encourage efficiency. *Controlled Reader* at recreational level.

Zintz:

Zintz mostly gives an immense list of materials to use in general remediation.

1 Write a paragraph using a beginners' dictionary.
2 The sight vocabulary is leaned by a *word* method.
3 The child:
   a) reads charts
   b) 'writes' experience stories
   c) sees labels in the room
   d) accomplishes workbook lessons
   e) does blackboard work
   f) drills with the teacher on a specific list of words
4 A basic reader is used to enlarge his sight vocabulary.
5 Word attack skills are developed at the same time.
6 The emphasis is on meaning.

Instructional Materials (Commercial)

When individual pupils or groups of pupils are deficient in word recognition skills, corrective practice can be individualized by using available commercial materials such as:

1 *Actions Picture- and Word-Making Game* (Philip & Tacey): Verbs are illustrated and separate word cards are matched through a self-corrective device. Individual letter cards for each word are also available.
2 *Bear Game* (Good Reading): Dial a word and its picture pops up. Try getting the children to guess the picture before dialling the chosen word.
3 *Beat the Clock* (E.J. Arnold): The words involved with this game are associated with food and contain some common combinations of letters which tend to pose problems in sight reading. They have self-checking pictures on the reverse side. Two games can be played with this set. The first, for one player, is similar to patience. The second game involves either one or two players.
4 *Colour Snap* (Good Reading): The two hundred picture-word cards can be sorted into five colour sets. The game of snap can be played by matching two pictures, two words, or a word and its picture. Pelmanism or Pairs can also be played with these cards.

5 *Elephant Game* (Good Reading): The picture-word cards are placed on the board, word uppermost. The elephant is spun until his trunk points to a word which must then be called. This call can be checked by the picture on the reverse side.
6 *Five First Steps and Pop Words* (Better Books): These instructional materials involve one hundred and fifty common sight or pop words printed in large, clear type on 10cm x 15cm cards. Consonant and vowel sounds are printed on coloured cards and include sixteen easy consonants, four consonant digraphs, the sounds of *y* and the hard and soft *c* and *g* sounds. (For use with individual children, children working in pairs, or with a group of children under proper direction.)
7 *Flash Cards* (Ladybird): Two sets each of one hundred and twenty double-sided word cards which cover more than half the words in common use. (For use with individual children, or the large set can be used with the whole class.)
8 *Flash X* (EDL) Educational Development Laboratories USA, distributed by Gateway Educational Media, Bristol: A tachistoscope (quick exposure device) consisting of a circular metal case and an aperture with a spring-loaded shutter, along with a series of card discs, both blank and with words. (For use by the teacher with individual children or by children working in pairs.)
9 *Heads and Tails Game* (E.J. Arnold): A self-corrective, competitive game involving picture and word matching. The game consists of a base board and forty-four picture-word cards. The words used present some of the more common phonic problems which can be difficult to read at sight. (For children working in pairs.)
10 *Key Words Reading Games Box* (Ladybird): A box containing sixteen different games which provide for extra practice and reinforcement of the words used in the Ladybird Keywords Reading Scheme. (There are different games for individuals, pairs, and small groups of children.)
11 *Keywords Self-Teaching Cards* (Galt): Each of two sets consists of four base boards (with eight words each) and

thirty-two picture cards with words on the back for matching and checking. (One to eight children can use these self-corrective cards).

12 *Linguistic Block Series* (Scott, Foresman): The first Rolling Reader (primer level) consists of a set of ten blocks involving fifty pre-primer and primer words; the second Rolling Reader (five-year-old level) consists of a set of ten blocks involving fifty-four verbs, nouns and adjectives; the third Rolling Reader (six-year-old level) consists of a set of ten blocks involving fifty-four auxiliary verbs and negative constructions. (For use with individual children, children working in pairs, or a small group of children.)

13 *Look, I'm Reading* (ESA): (i) Window Books — these books are arranged in matching paired sets:
   a) pictures of objects; open the page to reveal the word.
   b) words presented; open the page to reveal the matching picture.
   (ii) Lotto Game: Six picture boards and one hundred and twenty word cards for Bingo games. (For two to six players with a caller.)

14 *Mix and Match Dominoes* (Hart Davies): This self-corrective domino game gives practice in whole word recognition. There are six boxed sets of dominoes, each set using words relating to a specific theme. (For pairs of children or small groups.)

15 *Pictures and Words* (Blackie): This material (two teachers' display books and twelve pupils' books) provides pictures of everyday scenes which children can interpret and relate to the words which are printed alongside the display pictures. Each large display book consists of six pictures, each one corresponding to a pupils' book. (For small group or whole class work.)

16 *Picture-Word Lotto* (Galt): This new version of a well-known game extends the activity from simple picture matching to include sight word learning and word-to-word matching. There are four base boards and thirty-six picture cards. (For two to four players.)

17 *Picture-Word Matching Cards* (Galt): Picture-word cards have the word only on the reverse and separate word cards,

for playing many different games. The forty words which are used are grouped under four themes of interest to children: home, food, animals and transport.

18 *Spin and Win* (Good Reading): Children take it in turns to spin and read the word where the pointer stops. The pointer will hide the picture which goes with the word, until the pointer is moved to one side and the picture revealed. Other pictures and words can be stuck onto the board (For two or more players.)

19 *Time for Games* (Ginn): This box contains seven different board games which aid letter, word and sentence recognition. Each game is self-corrective. (For small groups of children.)

20 *Turn About* (Good Reading): A board game with word cards. Children throw a dice to decide which word is to be read, each card is self-checking with the appropriate picture on the reverse side. (For four players.)

Instructional Materials (teacher/pupil constructed)

When individual pupils or groups of pupils are deficient in word recognition skills, individualized practice can be provided by using teacher- or pupil-made materials such as the following (common sight vocabulary words are listed in Appendix A and Appendix B).

1 *Biscuit Tray Magnet:* Paste pictures of various objects on the inside surface of a shallow biscuit tray. Design matching word cards on the backs of which are glued small pieces of a bar magnet. The pupil engaged in this activity places words in proper position. The word cards are held in position by the pieces of bar magnet which adhere firmly to the metal of the biscuit tray. By numbering the pictures and the backs of the word cards, this activity can be made self-corrective. (For use with individual pupils, potentially self-directive.)

2 *Bowling:* Make a cardboard tachistoscope (quick exposure device) of a bowling pin. At the centre of the pin make an opening so words on coloured card can be seen by doing the following: print words to be learned on strips of coloured card and slip them behind the structure so they can

be exposed quickly, one at a time. If the child who starts can name ten words, he has made a strike and can try a new strip of words. (For use with two or more children.)

3   *Build—A—Train:* Engines and railway carriages are cut from coloured card. Each piece has a word printed or written on it. Children who pronounce the words correctly build a train which becomes longer. The object of the game is to see who can build the longest train. (For use with two or more children.)

4   *Card Method:* Each pupil is equipped with a small pile of cards (8cm x 13cm cards cut in half are fine). When an unknown word is encountered the pupil is instructed to write it on a card. The teacher, too, has cards in readiness at all times so any child in the reading circle who misses a word can be given an immediate written record of it. Several times a week the children are allowed to get together in groups of three for the purpose of quizzing each other on their cards. The chances are good that at least one of the three children will know a word. When all are uninformed, the teacher or a specially appointed assistant can provide the help needed. (For use with a group of children, potentially self-directive.)

5   *Carpenter:* Draw a picture of a house on a piece of heavy cardboard. Colour all but the roof. Paste art corners on the roof, about 4cm apart in even rows. On small cards about 1.5cm x 3cm print the words for drill. Each card is a tile. If a child can say the word, he can put it in the art corner and add a tile to the roof. If he does not know it, it falls to the ground. More than enough cards are given to the child so he can have reasonable success in completing the house. (For use with children working in pairs.)

6   *Draughts:* Buy a cheap draughtboard. Cut squares from masking tape that coincide in size with the draughtboard squares and place these on the squares where the draughts are to be placed or moved. Words are then printed on the masking tape right side up and upside down so both players can read any word appearing on the board. The game proceeds as a normal game of draughts, but a child must be able to read the word or words if he is to complete a move. If he fails to call the word correctly, he is told

what the word is. He must wait, however, until his next turn before attempting the move again. (For use with two children, potentially self-directive.)

7   *Classification:* Print in colour on individual cards two or more words that constitute categories such as *home* and *farm*. Place these in an envelope along with many other cards bearing words such as *kitchen, stove* and *barn*. The latter must be categorized under the two words printed in colour. By numbering the backs of the word cards, the exercise can be made self-corrective. (For use with individual children, potentially self-directive.)

8   *Colour Match:* Words pertaining to various colours are printed on pieces of card. Clothespegs that have been coloured are placed in an accompanying envelope. The child engaged in colour match shows his understanding of the words by attaching the appropriately coloured clothespegs to the word cards. By colouring the backs of the word cards with the colour named, this activity can be made self-corrective. (For use with individual children, potentially self-directive.)

9   *Fishing:* Word cards are cut from card in the shape of fish. A paper clip is slipped over each word card. Fishermen are equipped with a pole (short stick), a fishing line (50cm of string) and a fish hook (small magnet). Each child takes a turn trying to catch a fish. If he can read the word attracted to the magnet, he may keep the fish involved. If he doesn't know it he shows the word to the other children for a correct response and then returns it, face down, to the fish pond. (For use with two children or a group of children, potentially self-directive.)

10   *Jallopy Derby:* Make a four-car race track on as large a piece of cardboard as you can find. Divide the track into 8cm spaces and mark a starting line. Let the children make little cars of paper or buy little cars at a toy shop. On a small piece of card print the words you want the children to learn. A die is tossed for order of beginning. Number one then tosses the die for his first move. He may move as many spaces as the number on the die if he can say the word on the card he draws. If he cannot say the word, he loses his turn and the next child may use his word or pick a

new one. If he decides not to use the missed word, the next player may use it. If no one uses the missed word, it is put at the bottom of the pile. When the game is over special help is given with the missed words at the bottom of the pile. Each race is one lap. The winner is the one who comes out even with the finish line first. Should a potential winner throw a six and have only four or five spaces left, he may move just one space for the word he can say. Coming out even with the finish line adds excitement to the game. It gives each child a chance to become a last-minute winner. (For use with one, two, three or four children.)

11 *Match—A—Picture:* An ingeniously designed self-corrective exercise can be made by pasting a picture on a piece of card on the other side of which two matched and parallel columns of synonyms or antonyms have been written. The left-hand column is numbered from top to bottom so no difficulty can be experienced in arranging it properly at a later time. After this has been done the card is cut into individual word cards and the pieces are placed in a stiff manilla folder. The pupil who engages in this exercise begins by arranging the left-hand column as numbered. He then arranges in a parallel column the matching pieces. All the pieces involved are put in position inside the folder. When the pupil is ready to check his work, he closes the folder and flips it over. Upon opening the folder a complete picture appears. Any error manifests itself in a jumbled picture. (For use with individual pupils, potentially self-directive.)

12 *Matching:* Print words that designate specific colours *(sky, fire-engine, violets,* etc) on a sheet of coloured card. Place small cards of different colours in an attached envelope. The child matches the coloured cards with the words. By using an identification scheme on the backs of the colour cards, this activity can be made self-corrective. (For use with individual children, potentially self-directive.)

13 *Old Maid:* Print words on pieces of card the size of playing cards. Complete twenty cards and then make a duplicate set so twenty pairs of words result. Print one Old Maid card or, if you wish, one word alone may be used to designate to Old Maid card. Distribute the cards and begin with the person to the left of the dealer who starts the game by drawing a card from the person at his right. As pairs are formed, the words are called and placed on the table. This continues until all pairs are matched and one person holds the Old Maid. (For use with two to four children, potentially self-directive.)

14 *One Look Game:* Those words most frequently placed on cards are used with this activity. Pupils work in pairs with one child acting as a helper. The pack of cards is placed before the learner who picks up one card at a time, calls the word and then hands it to the helper. The helper retains those cards called correctly and segregates those called incorrectly. Any marked hesitation constitutes an error. When all cards have been called, the number of words missed is calculated and recorded in chart form. The helper then calls each word for the player who repeats aloud each word he has failed. The entire pack is reshuffled and is made ready for another 'one look' trial. (For use with children working in pairs.)

15 *Pairs:* This is a game similar to rummy and can be played by two to five children. Twenty-five words, each of which appears twice on playing cards, make a fifty-card deck. The object of the game is to get as many pairs as possible. When playing the game, five cards are dealt to each player and the remainder of the pack is placed face down on the table. The player to the right of the dealer begins by asking a fellow player for a specific card that will match one in his hand. If the latter has the card requested, he must give it up. If he does not have it the player draws one card from the pile and terminates his play. The player who gets the card for which he asks (should he not know the word he may solicit help from anyone present), either from another player or from the pile, has a second turn. As soon as a player has a pair, he places it on the table. The player with the most pairs wins.

16 *Pick—A—Chip:* Divide basic sight vocabulary words into four sections of fifty-five words each. Type or write the words on pieces of masking tape and place these on poker chips of four colours. Deposit the chips in four small boxes of matching colours. A pupil starts the game by choosing a

colour and then gives a spinner a whirl. He picks as many chips from his colour section as the spinner indicates. If he fails to say one of the words he is told what it is, but he must return the chip to the box and pass the spinner to the next player. The winner is the pupil who has acquired the most chips. (For use with three to four children.)

17 *Picture Checkerboard:* The teacher writes sixteen nouns on the board in numbered order. The children fold a sheet of drawing paper into sixteen squares and number them correspondingly. They then draw pictures of the nouns on the numbered squares. Later, papers can be exchanged and corrected. (For use with individual children or a group of children.)

18 *Picture Dictionary Match:* Paste pictures cut from an inexpensive dictionary in a row on a 23cm x 30cm card. Under each picture draw a space box 4cm x 1.5cm. Prepare small word cards and put these in an envelope which remains attached to the picture card. By numbering the pictures and the backs of the word cards, this activity can be made self-corrective. (For use with individual children, potentially self-directive.)

19 *Picture Riddle Matcho:* Children cut pictures from old magazines and place them in envelopes — five to an envelope. The teacher writes a riddle about one of the pictures and places it in the envelope with the pictures. The child who chooses the envelope selects the picture which answers the riddle. A marking scheme can be devised to make this activity self-corrective. (For use with individual children, potentially self-directive.)

20 *Ring—A Word:* Utilize heavy plywood in constructing a board 60cm x 90cm in size. Arrange five nails on the board and paint numbers from one to five under the nails. Print words on small cards and hang them on the nails. (Easiest cards should be on number one nail and hardest cards on number five nail.) Equip children with a box of rubber jar rings. The directions for the game are 'ring a word and score the points if you can say it'. (For use with two or more children.)

21 *Shoestring Matcho:* Two rows of mixed synonyms or an antonym row and synonym row are written side by side in columns. A hole should be made next to each word between the columns, and shoestrings attached to the right of the first row by knotting the ends on the reverse side. The child indicates the correct answer by slipping the shoestring into the correct hole in front of words in the second column. A marking scheme can be devised on the reverse side to make this activity self-corrective. (For use with individual children, potentially self-directive.)

22 *Tachistoscope:* Let a child find a picture that interests him or her. Mount his picture on card and cut two horizontal slits 4cm long and 1cm apart. Words to be learned are printed or typed on strips of coloured card about 4cm wide. The strips are then inserted in the slits and pulled through so one word is exposed at a time. (For use with children working in pairs.)

23 *Word Basketball:* Remove the top and one of the long sides of a packing carton. Use green and white paint to give what resembles the appearance of a basketball court. Baskets can be simulated by pasting two small paper bags on the outside of the box. If a player can call correctly a word he has drawn from a word pile, he pushes the word card through a slot above his team's basket and his side gets two points. If he calls incorrectly, someone on the other team tries. A referee will determine if the word is said correctly or not. The score can be kept by counting the number of cards in each bag. (For use with two children or two groups of children under proper direction.)

24 *Word Authors:* Words are printed on corners of cards — four cards to a set. A set may consist of four colours, four animals, four synonyms and the like. Each child is dealt four cards and one child begins the game by calling for a word. If he gets the word, he may continue to call for words. When his opponent indicates that he does not have the card called for, the child draws from the deck of cards that is face down on the table. The child who acquires the most sets wins. (For use with two to four children, potentially self-directive.)

25 *Word File Pictures:* The name of an object is printed at the top of the card, and a picture or drawing is placed below to illustrate it. On the opposite side of the cards just the word is printed. The child tries to read the word and then checks his response by looking at the picture on the front side of the card. (For use with individual children, potentially self-directive.)

26 *Wordo:* The teacher with the help of her children prepares cardboard master cards 20cm x 28cm in size. These master cards are marked off into twenty-five small squares. The middle space is marked *free*. Individual words that are troublesome are placed on the twenty-four squares that remain. Each cardboard master card must have the same words but in different positions. The twenty-four words are typed or printed on small cards and placed in an envelope. As individual words are drawn from the envelope and called aloud, the players find the words on their master cards and cover them with a marker of some sort. The marker may be a bean or a small piece of cardboard etc. The first child to cover a row of words in a straight line, vertically, horizontally or diagonally, calls out 'wordo'. If he is correct, he is declared the winner. (For use with two or more children, potentially self-directive.)

Problem 2 Inadequate Visual Analysis Skills

2 Inadequate Visual Analysis Skills

The child should be able to separate words into parts that are going to be useful to him in recognizing the words. He must be flexible in this skill so that if he finds his method of dividing the words is unsuitable then he can quickly re-appraise the words and re-analyse them. He should select the largest usable elements. Some children tend to consistently make mistakes in a specific part of words: the inital part, the middle part, or the end of the word. Exercises should be given which focus the child's attention upon the part of the word which he tends to overlook. He should be encouraged to inspect words in an orderly fashion. The use of context as a check on accuracy will encourage the child to re-inspect the words missed.

Possible Causes

1 Faulty approach to word recognition such as letter-by-letter spelling or sounding.
2 Limited knowledge of vowel sounds.
3 Hurried inspection of unfamiliar words to point where middles are neglected.
4 Neglect of/or overdependence on context.
5 Dependence on one technique, or use of the most inefficient ones.

Signs of Disability

1 Neglects to notice beginnings or endings of words closely (says *this* as *his*, *the* as *he*, *tall* as *fall*, *talk* as *tall*, etc.).
2 A child with this disability will select inappropriate parts to sound out and often he will try again and again to use the same analysis when it has proven ineffective.
3 Vowel confusions (*hut, hot, hit, hat*).

4 Confusion of words of several syllables which have similar beginnings and endings (*commission* and *communion, precision* and *procession*).
5 Fails to note or discriminate endings as —s, —es, —ly, —est, —er, —ness.
6 Is unable to recognize a word when someone divides it into parts for him.
7 Poor in visual analysis sections of diagnostic tests.
8 Poor in syllabication skills of visual analysis tests.

Remedial Work

1 The child should be taught to use the words which are familiar to him to help identify unknown words by noting their similarities.
2 Readers at the child's level of attainment and their manuals provide excellent material for this instruction because their basic vocabulary is controlled and words are repeated at convenient intervals. Manuals accompanying basic reading programmes give many suggestions for introducing new vocabulary. The teacher is not only supposed to make the meaning clear, but is also expected to show the child the most efficient visual analysis of each word and compare it, when necessary, with known words which contain the element causing the child's difficulty. All exercises should be in contextual settings because often the pronunciation of a word depends upon its use in the particular sentence or story.
3 Move to materials that are more difficult so that the child will be forced to analyse words visually. Useful exercises are those which deal with compound words, root words, with variant endings, suffixes, prefixes and syllabication.

Sample Exercises:

1 Multiple choice questions in which the child is forced to attend to the initial element.

boat

The man put on his goat.

coat

2 Classification exercises that emphasize initial sounds and word meanings.

Find every word that starts like 'can' and is something we can eat.

crab	corn	bread
apple	clown	creep

3 Multiple choice exercises in which the initial blend is given.

The car went down the str_____ .

strange	road	street

4 Multiple choice exercises which focus attention on the middle elements.

pen

a) The pig was in the pan.

pin

children

b) The chimp   came out of the egg.

chicken

5 Exercises for focusing the attention on the final element.

a) Finish the word. It should rhyme with 'call'.
The boy was playing with the b _____ .

tall	back	ball

b) Find the words which end like 'coat' which you would like to play with.

goat	doll	float
gloat	boat	clock

6 Exercises to teach variant endings.

Draw a line under the right word.

drink

The cat   her milk.

drinks

7 Exercises to teach common word elements.

Put in the right word. It must end like the word 'light'.
It was a dark _____ .

right	room	night

See how many words you can make that rhyme with the following words. Use each in a sentence.

steep	bright	house

8 Exercises which involve finding the root word in words with variant ending forms.

Find the root words from which these words are made.

looks	looking	looked
worker	worked	working
washes	washing	washed

9 Exercises which involve making choices between variant forms.

wanting

The bear   the honey.

wanted

10 Exercises which involve finding similar blends.

You see the picture of the clown and say clown. Look at the words here and put an X on the ones that begin like clown and tell something you can do.

clap	clean	clocks
come	clothes	play
climb	cook	clam

11 Exercises that emphasize seeing similar word parts.

a) Put an X on the right word:
She wanted to _____ for joy.

shell	shout	shoe

b) Draw a line under the right word:
The sun cannot be seen at _____ .

fight	night	right	sight

12 Exercises that teach syllabication.

a) Say the words below and think how many parts you hear. These parts are syllables. Write the number of syllables after each word.

about __	surprise __	something __

b) Show the syllables in these words (e.g. ab/sol/ute).

ahead	forgotten	furniture

13 Exercises that emphasize seeing the two parts of compound words.

> Find the two small words in each compound word and tell how they help us know what it means.
>
> fireplace   baseball   sailboat   policeman

14 Exercises that develop skill in analysing affixed words.

  a) Draw a line around the part of the word that means 'again'.

> relive   remake   retell

  b) Draw a line around the prefix and tell how it changes the meaning of the root word.

> unhappy   retake   displease

  c) Draw a line around the suffix in these words. Put the right number after the words to show the meaning of the suffix.

> thoughtless   slowly   tasteful
> full of (1)   without (2)   in that way (3)

  d) Draw a line around the root word, the word from which the larger word is made. Tell how the prefix and suffix change the meaning of the root word.

> unfriendly   disagreeable   repayable

Syllabication:

The child is given a list of common words. He divides the words into syllables.

The child is given a list of words. He underlines words ending in a certain syllable such as -ight and -ing.

The child is given a series of pictures. He names each object pictured and writes the number of syllables in the name under the picture.

A list of words is given to the child. He indicates the number of syllables in each word.

The child is given the rules governing syllabication together with a list of words. He divides the words into syllables and indicates which rule he used.

Suffixes:

A list of words containing suffixes is given to the child. He identifies the root word in each word.

The child is given a list of words containing suffixes. He uses the root word in a sentence.

The child is given a list of unknown words. He separates the suffix from the word and pronounces both suffix and root word.

The child is given a list of words with definitions after each word. He adds one of a given group of suffixes to the words so the newly formed word complies with the definition after the word.

The child is given a list of words. He makes new words by adding a given suffix to the words on the list.

Prefixes:

The child is given a list of words. He writes a given prefix before the words and gives the meaning of the new words.

A series of sentences with one word missing in each is given to the child. He fills in the words using the correct prefixes.

A group of prefixes and a list of words with definitions are given to the child. He adds one of the prefixes from the group to each word so it corresponds to the definition written after each word.

A list of words with prefixes is given to the child. He writes the words without the prefix and indicates how the meaning has been changed.

The child is given a list of unknown words with a known prefix. He finds the meaning of the new word.

The child is given a list of words with prefixes. He underlines the prefixes.

The child is given a list of words containing common prefixes. He underlines the root word.

Common Compound Words:

A list of compound words is given to the child. He draws a line between the two words making up each compound word.

Two columns of words are given to the child. He makes compound words by matching the words in one column with the words in the other column.

The child is given a list of compound words. He writes the two short words that make up the compound beside each word.

The child is given two lists of words. He combines words from the two lists to form single compound words.

Endings of Words:

A series of phrases is given to the child. If a phrase refers to more than one, the child makes the subject of the phrases plural.

The child is given a group of pictures. The child names the objects in the pictures and gives the plural of the name if there is more than one object involved.

The child is given a list of singular words. He forms the plurals of each word in the list.

The child is given a list of words. He forms new words by adding given endings to the words.

Teaching suggestions

The following suggestions are drawn from the work of reading specialists. Sources are listed under the authors' names in the bibliography.

Betts:

1 Use discovery technique with groups of words having the same prefix. Direct attention to the similarities in meaning due to the prefix; e.g. unknown, unkind, unload.
2 Give a direct explanation to words requested by pupils in the course of their reading.
3 Identify root words and affixes in words.
4 List antonyms of words by using affixes.
5 Build a list of words based on several root words.
6 Match affixes and meanings.
7 *Rewriting sentences:* The pupils are given a number of sentences containing words with prefixes or suffixes. They are instructed to identify the word with a prefix and rewrite each sentence with a new word or phrase to give the same idea.
    Example:
       Mary returned my book.
       Mary brought back my book.
    Another use of rewording sentences to call attention to prefixes and suffixes may be made this way.

Example:
   Bob was proud to ride his new bicycle.
   Bob proudly rode his new bicycle.

8 *Forming compounds:* The teacher may have the children form compounds from a list of words selected from their reading vocabulary.
    Example: Draw a line between each pair of words that
            make a compound word.
            under   thing
            any   day
            some   out
            with   stand

Bond and Tinker:

Emphasize beginning of words.

Building picture dictionaries; alphabetizing exercises; sorting labelled pictures for filing.

Exercises: initial consonant blends; digraphs; multiple-choice questions in which attention is on initial element; classification that emphasizes initial sounds and word meanings; multiple-choice exercises in which initial blend is given.

Help the child locate the most useful structural, visual and phonic elements in words; to develop flexibility in visual attack on words teach the use of large elements first.

Exercises: finding root word in words with variant endings; making choices between variant forms; finding similar blends; seeing similar word parts; syllabication; seeing two parts of compound words; analysing affixed words.

Exercises that teach the phonic sounds of vowels.

Methods that encourage inspecting words in orderly way.

Copying words or tracing words that cause difficulty.

Using context as a check on accuracy.

Dechant:

Point out that substituting one final consonant for another completely changes the word; for example:

   Bob wants a pe*t*.   Bob wants a pe*n*.

Della-Piana:

1 Words are introduced gradually and revised extensively.

2 Teach child to observe configuration and obvious component features. Later, teach how to observe more details, to observe more quickly and accurately, to work out recognition of unfamiliar words, and to acquire familiarity with new words in terms of these visual elements.

3 Gates — have student close eyes and see in his mind's eye the word he has observed. He is encouraged to see it part by part, in the left-to-right order, and then as a whole. If the word can be divided into syllables, he is asked to say them softly to himself while visualizing them simultaneously. Later, as he learns to write, he is asked to visualize the syllables as he writes and sounds them.

Drummond and Wignell:

Phonic development — blends, consonant clusters, vowel and consonant digraphs.
Structural analysis — word endings, plurals, compounds, possessives, contraction, syllabication.
(The above drills are always directed towards the meaning of the word in context.)

Durrell:

Give specific practice in visual perception by showing words on flash cards, on a board, on a tachistoscope.
Exercises in word groupings to force attention on particular word elements; general structure; initial letter; word endings; elements within the word.
Drill on pronouncing useful words.
Syllable study of words that follow regular phonics patterns.
Counting syllables in words.
Identifying visual forms of sound elements in words.
Encourage auditory and visual analysis of words. Child must be able to distinguish sounds within the word.
Practise visual analysis skills in spelling lessons.
Practise syllables, root words, compound words, blends and phonograms.
Select from a number of words, having similar elements, the only one that fits the pronunciation of a word.

Write word after seeing word flashed.
Use lists composed of troublesome words in recent lessons and/or words that will appear in future lessons.
Use paragraphs in which inflectional endings are omitted. Child reads and adds required endings.
Expand a known word by adding endings.
Use rhyming words that fit context.
Match words in lists that rhyme.
Use a systematic kinaesthetic procedure with some children.

Gilliland:

Practise with a tachistoscope.
Play games requiring letter discrimination.
Use kinaesthetic tracing.
Overlearn several letters at a time.
Write 'mixed up' letters on the board and have the pupils name them aloud.
Teach prefixes, endings, and common letter clusters.
Check visual memory and if it is poor do not force the student to change his reading habits suddenly.

Harris:

Teach common phonograms which combine with initial consonants to form many different words.
Correct reversal tendencies and weakness in word recognition.
Emphasize noticing the beginning of words.
Give exercises in alphabetizing and the use of dictionaries.
Provide practice in discriminating vowels; lists of words which are alike except for the median vowel; words which are different except for the same median vowel.
Give training in use of context.
Teach how to attack words systematically, syllable by syllable.
Point out how the ending changes the meaning of a word.
Give practice in sentences which force selection of word with right ending.

Heilman:

Help children to analyse words by:
word form or the unique appearance of words
structural analysis
context clues
phonic analysis
methods in combination
Review and extend child's experience with common word endings, compound words, doubling consonants before adding endings beginning with a vowel, adding *es* to form some plurals, forming plurals of words ending with *y*, contractions, recognizing prefixes and suffixes adding to root words, syllabication.
Use kinaesthetic tracing method, or visual-motor method with severely impaired readers or with any children who consistently confuse certain words or who reverse words.

Kottmeyer:

Determine if child knows letters by sight. Check also his knowledge of the sounds of letters.
Use picture card drill in which child says or writes beginning sound.
Teach and give practice with words beginning with *sh, ch, th, wh.*
Stress that these letter combinations have only one sound.
Give practice in consonants that have more than one sound; e.g. hard and soft *c, g.*
Use word wheels for practice.
Child must have acquired adequate sight vocabulary in order that initial consonant substitution may be helpful. To acquire skill in consonant substitution child must have power of visual imagery to recall known word.
Give practice adding various endings to known words.

Otto and McMenemy:

Common cause of error is due to vowel confusion.
Give practice with words differing only in vowel sound.
Progress to words in which other letters change and vowel remains the same.
Teach orderly inspection of words.

Money:

Emphasize features which are actually distinctive for letters by presenting letters in contrast pairs.
Use colour phonics system for dyslexic children.
Use techniques for 'visual dictation' with words in colour.

Russell:

A combined method of word attack (both phonic and structural) should be used.
He has prepared an outline indicating how phonic and structural analyses are gradually combined in a word analysis programme.

Tinker and McCullough:

Give exercises in initial consonant sounds; consonant substitution, consonant blends.
Teach common prefixes.
Give exercises in single vowel sounds, vowel sounds, vowel digraphs, and diphthongs.
Give ear training for vowel sounds.
Teach inflectional endings.
Teach phonograms or rhyme endings.

Instructional Materials (Commercial)

When individual pupils or groups of pupils are deficient in visual analysis skills, corrective practice can be individualized by using available commercial material such as:

1 *ABC Game* (Better Books): A game that aids in teaching letter, word, and picture recognition. Twenty-six pairs of cards having capitals on one card and small letters on the matching card are involved. The object of the game is to find the mate for every card in each player's hand. (For use with two to four children, potentially self-directive.)

2 *Approach Picture and Word-Building Cards* (Philip & Tacey): Five boxes each containing picture-word cards, one box for each short vowel a, e, i, o and u. Picture matching, word matching and letter matching activities are possible with this apparatus.

3 *Combination Form-a-Word Kit* (Better Books): Four sets of flip cards for making words; word blend, prefix, suffix and syllable flip cards.

4 *Debden Suffix Changing Cards* (Philip & Tacey): This material consists of six base cards with cut-outs and four sets of eight suffix cards for word-making. Additional sentence cards are available which make use of both forms of each word in a sentence.

5 *Five First Steps and Pop Words* (Better Books): This instructional material involves one hundred and fifty common sight or pop words printed in large, clear type on 10cm x 15cm cards. Consonant and vowel sounds are printed on coloured cards and include sixteen easy consonants, four consonant digraphs, the sounds of *y* and the hard and soft *c* and *g* sounds. (For use with individual children, children working in pairs or with a group of children under proper direction.)

6 *Groundwork Key Words and Pictures Material* (Philip & Tacey): There are seventy-two pictures each illustrating a comprehensive range of consonant and vowel digraphs. These are accompanied by ninety-six single word cards which have a single letter or digraph on one side and on the reverse the word which shows the vowel or digraph in red. Word panels display three words with the appropriate digraph printed in red. (This material is valuable for small groups or class work.)

7 *Happy Words* (Macdonald): This 'Happy Families' game, based on collecting picture-word cards sharing the same initial consonant letter clusters, helps the child to recognize the letter grouping as they all appear on each card for each family, and are always grouped together — thus seen together. (For three, four or five players.)

8 *Letter Discrimination Inset Boards* (Philip & Tacey): A set of two boxes, each containing two base boards, which offer letter-matching activities. The fourteen single letters or letter pairs on the boards have insets where their corresponding cards are to be placed.

9 *Letter Recognition and Sorting Strip Books* (Philip & Tacey): In the first four books the activity is limited to matching three single letters, each on a separate strip. In the second four books groups of two letters are provided for matching in sets of three.

10 *Liguistic Block Series* (Scott Foresman): Rolling phonics, consonants: consists of a set of ten blocks involving eleven one-syllable words beginning with vowels and twelve consonants or consonant blends. Over eighty-five words can be built. (For use with individual children, children working in pairs, or a small group of children.)

11 *Look, I'm Reading* (ESA): Alphabet Cards — A set of laminated cards which can be hung on the wall or used flat on the desk. There is one card for each letter of the alphabet. Five words are printed on each card with five pictures. Each card has a pocket at one end which contains three cards for each of the five words displayed; one with the picture only, one with the word alone, and one with the picture and the word.

12 *Look Visual Perception Material* (Macmillan): Four pupils' workbooks provide plenty of practice for perceptual readiness and development for the visual discrimination of letter and word differences.

13 *Make-a-Word Spelling Game* (Philip & Tacey): This apparatus consists of two sets of base cards which include pictures and words, and the words have matching letter cards. Children work in pairs on separate base cards to complete their words by covering each word with the appropriate letter cards.

14 *Match-It* (Hart Davis): Twelve sets of four picture-word cards are placed face down on the table. The word endings are underlined, and pairs have to be collected by playing the game called Memory or Pelmanism. (For two, three or four players.)

15 *Oxford Picture- and Word-Building Cards* (Philip & Tacey): Each of four boxes contains ten word and picture cards together with the appropriate letter cards. The loose letters are used by the child to reconstruct the word.

16 *Phonic Sets* (Hart Davis): This pack of forty-eight cards consists of twelve sets of four word cards which begin with the same consonant letter group. The game is played like rummy to collect the sets of four. (For two, three or four players.)

17 *Picture-Letter Dominoes* (Galt): Letters and Pictures-and-Letters are matched to play the traditional dominoes game. Only initial letters are used. (For two or more players.)

18 *Spin-and-Spell Spelling Game* (Philip & Tacey): A simple spelling game in which the word cards are handed out, the letter-selector spun, and letters chosen to complete the words in each player's possession. (For two or more players.)

19 *Syllaboscope and Related Word Set* (Better Books): A system by which the pupil can be taught syllable division and the construction of words. The syllaboscope has wooden partitions to block off certain parts of a word.

20 *Vowel and Digraph Word Completion Slides* (Philip & Tacey): This apparatus presents the child with a visual means of completing words by inserting the missing vowel or digraph. Each of four boxes consists of one plastic channel, four picture-word strips and four vowel or digraph transparent plastic slides.

21 *Word Change* (Galt): This game gives practice in word change caused by final *e*. The set consists of twenty-five three-letter picture-word cards with additional small *e* letters and twenty-five four-letter picture-word cards.

22 *Word Prefixes* (Better Books): A set of subdivided folding cards that highlight prefixes that blend to form two hundred and sixteen words. The meaning of each prefix is given and the words being shown are keyed on the back of each card. (For use with individual children, children working in pairs or a group of children.)

23 *Word Slides* (Longman): The Level 1 cards in this programme call for visual discrimination between pairs of words to match a single picture. Each card is self-corrective.

24 *Word Suffixes* (Better Books): A set of subdivided, folding cards that highlight twenty-four word endings. A total of one hundred and forty-four words are formed. The meaning of each suffix is given and words being shown are keyed in small type. (For use with individual children, children working in pairs, or a small group of children.)

Instructional Materials (Teacher/Pupil Constructed)

When individual pupils or groups of pupils are deficient in visual analysis skills, individualized practice can be provided by using teacher- or pupil-made materials such as the following:

1 *Arrange—O:* Place in an envelope a large picture of an object, starting with an initial consonant sound you are teaching. In another envelope, place small pictures of objects, some of which begin with the sound involved. The child arranges the appropriate pictures in a column under the master picture. By using an identification scheme on the back of the pictures, this activity can be made self-corrective. (For use with individual children, potentially self-directive.)

2 *Baseball:* A baseball diamond is drawn on the blackboard or on cardboard. Two group of children are chosen. The pitcher flashes a letter. If the batter calls a word beginning with the letter, he has made a hit and moves to first base. Should the next batter score a hit also, he moves to first base and the first batter advances to second. Soon the runs begin to come in. Teams change sides just as soon as three outs (wrong answers) have been given. The team with the most runs wins. (For use with groups of children.)

3 *Clothespeg Wheel:* Cut out a circular piece of coloured card about 30cm in diameter. Paste or draw pictures of common objects around the periphery of the card. Equip the child with a box of clothespegs on each of which is printed an initial consonant. The child then matches the clothespegs with the proper pictures. For example, the *c* clothespeg over the picture of a cat; the *p* clothespeg over the picture of a pear. (For use with individual children, potentially self-directive.)

4 *Consonant Fishing:* Consonant cards are cut in the shape of a fish. A paper clip is slipped over each card. Fishermen are equipped with a pole (short stick) a fishing line (50cm of string) and fish hook (small magnet). Each child takes a turn trying to catch fish. If he can call a word that begins with the consonant sound on the fish he has caught, he may keep the fish. If he is unable to think of a suitable word, he returns the fish face down to the fishpond. (For use with two children or a group of children, potentially self-directive.)

5 *Consonant Lotto:* The teacher, with the help of the children, prepares cardboard master cards 20cm x 28cm in size. These master cards are blocked off vertically and horizontally into twenty-five small squares. The middle space is marked *free*. Individual letters and digraphs are placed on the twenty-four spaces that remain. Each cardboard master card must have the same letters but in different positions. Twenty-four words known by the children on sight that begin with the individual letters or consonant digraphs involved are placed in an envelope. As individual words drawn from the envelope are called, the players find the beginning letter of the digraph on their master cards and cover it with a marker. The marker may be a kernel of corn, a bean, or a small piece of cardboard. The first child to cover a row of letters in a straight line, vertically, horizontally or diagonally, calls out 'lotto'. If he is correct he is declared the winner. (For use with two children or a group of children, potentially self-directive.)

6 *Happy Ending:* This is a structural analysis game consisting of one hundred and eight playing cards divided into eleven units of eight cards, and one unit of twelve cards labelled *Perfect Fit*. A third unit (four cards) is labelled *Wait* and four cards are labelled *Surprise*. The first eleven units have eight different words with the same ending. The ending is printed in colour.

The cards are shuffled and eleven cards are dealt to each player. The remaining cards are put into a pack in the centre of the table. The top card is turned face up next to the deck and starts the discarded pile.

Anyone having a *Surprise* card in this hand places it on the table face up in front of him and immediately draws another card from the pack. The player to the left of the dealer begins playing. He will draw the card turned up or draw from the top of the deck. If he draws the turned up card, he must be able to use it immediately either in a triangle or on a triangle. (A triangle is three or more cards with the same ending put down face up in front of the player.) A player may add to any triangle that he or she has on the table. A triangle of three cards may have one *Perfect Fit* in it. It is important that each card played on the table is read. If a player cannot read the triangle or an individual card, his partner can attempt to read them. If neither can read the card or cards, a monitor may tell the player, but he must keep it or them in his hand until his next turn.

A player terminates his play by putting a card on the discard pile and reading it. If a player needs assistance in reading this card he discards it. The playing continues clockwise around the table. One person in the partnership keeps the cards in front of him, and his partner plays on them or adds to the 'lay down'. As the playing continues, the player who wants the top card of the discard pile for playing on a triangle or in a triangle must take all the cards in the pile and read and play the top one immediately.

Perfect Fit can be used as any card and help to make three or more of a kind. A *Wait* card on a discarded pile *stops* the discard pile for the next player who then must draw from the unused pack. A *Happy Ending* is made when seven cards with the same ending have been played. This may include the *Perfect Fits*; however, only three *Perfect Fits* can be used in one *Happy Ending*.

The game is over when a player has a *Happy Ending* and is rid of all the cards in his hand. The player will try to get as many *Happy Endings* as he can

Scoring is as follows: A *Happy Ending* counts 100; going out counts 50; *Surprise* counts 50; *Perfect Fit* counts 10, every other card counts 5. The score of all the cards left in the hands of the other players when a player goes out is subtracted from his score on the table. The remaining score for each couple is added and tallied. The couple who first attains a score of 1,000 is declared winner. (For use with two sets of partners.)

7 *Matching Letter and Objects:* The teacher pastes a number of small pictures on a sheet of coloured card. (A flannel board, if available, might be used.) The pictures should be of things the children can recognize easily. An envelope containing a number of consonants is clipped to the sheet of card. The children remove the consonant cards and place them on or below the appropriate pictures. By use of an identification scheme on the backs of the cards, this activity can be made self-corrective. (For use with individual children, potentially self-directive.)

8 *Pockets:* Obtain some cheap envelopes and mount them on a chart as pockets for 8cm x 13cm cards. A consonant is printed on each envelope. The cards have pictures or drawings on them which are to be placed in the pockets beginning with the appropriate consonant sound. By using an identification scheme on the backs of the cards, this activity can be made self-corrective. (For use with individual children, potentially self-directive.)

9 *Spin and Call:* Divide a large coloured card circle into eight sections. Place a consonant in each section. Attach a large pointer to the centre of the circle so it spins freely. The player spins the pointer and calls a word beginning with the particular consonant to which it points when coming to a stop. If a correct word is called, he scores a point. A record should be kept of the words so no repetitions take place. (For use with two children or a group of children.)

10 *Taxi:* With the help of children build a little village of letters beside each of which is a small paper house. There can be several streets in Alphabet Village. Tall Street can consist of those letters which extend above the line (*b, d, f, h, k, l* and *t*); Low Street can consist of those letters which extend below the line (*j, p* and *g*); Friends Street of those letters that go together to make a sound (*ch, sh, th* and *wh*) Vowel Street of the vowels; Main Street of any letters left over.

One child acts as taxi driver. The other children ask the driver to take them to any word they want. The driver has to 'drive' them to the house whose letter starts the word. (For use with a group of children.)

11 *Toss Game:* With the use of alphabet blocks or building blocks on which initial consonants have been painted, children can take turns rolling blocks and giving words beginning with the letters that come up. (For use with two or more children, potentially self-directive.)

12 *Word Authors:* Words are printed on corners of cards — four cards to a set. A set consists of four words beginning with the same consonant. Each child is dealt four cards. One child begins the game by calling for a card beginning with a certain initial consonant sound. If he gets the word, he may continue to call for words. When his opponent indicates that he does not have the card called, the child draws from the deck of cards that is face down on the table. The child who acquires the most sets wins. (For use with two or four children, potentially self-directive.)

13 *What am I?:* On individual cards write riddles which give initial sounds as clues. For example, 'I am a tree-climbing animal. I have a long tail and like to swing from branches with it. I begin with the *m* sound. What am I?' Each child in the group has a chance at a riddle card. If he guesses the answer he is given the card. The child with the largest number of cards is the winner. By placing the answers on the backs of the cards this activity can be made self-corrective. (For use with a group of children, potentially self-directive.)

14 *Word Flight:* This is a structural analysis game consisting of fifty-two playing cards on each of which is a two-, three-, or four-syllable word. The difficulty of the game can be increased by having many multiple-syllable words.

The playing board is constructed by placing a mimeo-graphed map of Britain on cardboard. Railway routes should be drawn between major towns. Miniature trains of different colours should be made for use by each player.

To begin playing, the deck of cards is placed in the centre of the table near the playing board. Each player draws his first card from the centre deck. The player who draws a word with the least number of syllables is the first to play. If he has a one-syllable word, he may travel to the first town on the route. If he has a two-syllable word, he travels to the second town and so forth. Each player in turn draws a card, says the word on the card, tells how many syllables are in the word and moves his train along the route. If he cannot say the word or determine the number of syllables in it, someone tells him, but he cannot move his train. The player who reaches the home field first wins the game. (For use with two to four children, potentially self-directive.)

3 Inadequate Auditory Analysis Skills

3 Inadequate Auditory Analysis Skills

The child must be able to apply phonic analysis to both easy and difficult words. The purpose of these phonic skills is the recognition of unknown words in meaningful context.

Possible Causes

1 Lacks auditory acuity.
2 Lack of phonics training.
3 Child was not ready for phonics training.
4 Deficiencies in instruction — child learned sounds of letters and memorized rules without being shown how to apply them.

Signs of Disability

1 Auditory deficiency.
2 Confuses letter names with letter sounds.
3 Unable to blend sounds in working out pronunciations.
4 Fails to recognize new words.
5 Difficulty in spelling.
6 Cannot sound out words.
7 Does not know how to 'attack' polysyllabic words.

Remedial Work

1 Begin with consonant sounds, then vowels, and then on to blends, digraphs, etc. Use small words known to the child to establish principles that can be applied to a large number of words.
2 Teach the child to be aware of 'exceptions to the rule' in phonic work. Integrate with work on sight vocabulary.
3 Use context to verify all phonetically analysed words.

Sample Exercises:

1 Exercises in substituting initial sounds. Choose the right word.

> I can see a _____ car.
> bed   red

2 Exercises in substituting final sounds. Choose the right word.

> The _____ has a kitten.
> cat   can

3 Exercises in substituting medial vowels. Choose the right word.
a) The girl was _____ .
> set   sad
b) I will _____ a cake.
> back   bake
c) The boat has a _____ .
> lake   leak

4 *1, 2, 3 Practice.* Teacher places three words dealing with a similar phonic element on a card and puts the numbers 1, 2, 3 underneath.

> Example: fat   bat   sat
>   1   2   3

Teacher then asks the children which word is '____' (pronounces one of the words.) Children must respond by holding up the correct number on a separate card. An alternative form of this drill is for the teacher to ask the children to complete a sentence using one of the three words.

Teaching Suggestions

The following suggestions are drawn from the work of reading specialists. Sources are listed under the authors' names in the bibliography.

Dechant:

Before using blends in reading, the teacher should work with very simple sentences or even words.

Cards containing the blends and a picture of an object whose name contains the appropriate sound help to consolidate these sounds.

The pupil should do exercises which require him to join a consonant blend to one or more of the endings.

Picture of object shown without consonant blend, child fills in consonant blend.

The pupil must learn to recognize the various *al (ol)* combinations as in *all, stall, sold,* etc. Also, the *ar* combinations *(garb, lard, scarf,* etc.) and *short a* sounds *(fast, gasp,* etc.) must be learned.

Durrell:

Stages in phonic development:
1 auditory training
2 knowledge of letter forms and names
3 knowledge of letter sounds
4 practice in word analysis
5 use of context clues
6 refinement of phonic skills
7 translation of words into ideas

'Sounding out' words should be done when words are regular in sound, are within child's vocabulary, and apply immediately in the next reading lesson.

Build words that match pictures.

Build compound words.

Give word-building practice.

Make rhyming words.

Auditory discrimination of sound should precede visual presentation.

Need not have complete mastery of all sounds before beginning development of sight vocabulary.

Practise visual discrimination in printed symbols.

Harris:

Give ear and eye training: start with practice in listening for the sound within known words.

Give known words containing the phonic element.

Have comparisons made with words that sound similar but do not contain the phonic element, and with those words that look similar but do not contain it.

Provide vivid association which can be used to recall the sound: picture cues; dramatizing sounds; tracing and writing the letter for reinforcement; continuing story method.

Give preliminary training in auditory discrimination.

Heilman:

Teach:

Auditory discrimination of speech sounds in words.

A number of sight words — since all following steps are based on child's knowing sight words.

Sounds of initial consonants in words which have been learned as sight words.

Mental substitution of initial consonants.

Substitution of final consonants.

Initial consonant blends.

Vowel sounds.

Silent consonants.

Syllabication.

Kottmeyer:

Teach consonant substitution so that context will give clue to new words.

Child should know generalizations regarding phonics.

Child must be able to hear sounds in words. Begin with words that are phonetically regular.

Introduce consonant sounds first. Teach a key word for each.

Use left to right sequence with blending sounds to prevent reversal tendencies.

Consonant sounds and symbols show consistency 98% of the time; vowels, about 80%.

Teach new phonic skills with word child knows orally.

Money

Gillingham technique:
Present phonic units on separate cards.
Consonants on white cards.
Vowels on salmon-coloured cards.
Phonemes for spelling on buff cards.
Each phonogram is introduced by a key word.
The letter sounds are taught in groups as rapidly as they can be assimilated.
First group — letters with only one sound, non-reversible forms.
After the names of the letters and their sounds have been learned, the blending process is started: a consonant card, a vowel card, and another consonant card are laid on the table — pupil is taught to give their sounds rapidly and smoothly until he is producing a word.

The Colour Phonics System:
Uses a letter case or composing box, with a small mirror for the pupil to see his lips and tongue.
Vowels are printed in red and arranged in compartments along lower edge of box.
Pupil learns that there must always be a red letter in a word.
Upper section of box contains consonants and is divided into three areas — lip sounds, front tongue sounds and throat sounds.
Begin instruction with phonetically regular words and short sentences.

Otto & McMenemy:

Give a lot of practice in auditory perception. Child must be able to recognize differences and similarities of sounds in initial, final and medial positions.
When blending sounds, time between letters should be almost imperceptible.
Present entire word and then proceed to analyse individual sounds.

Teaching order is:
single-sound consonants
consonant blends
consonant digraphs (*ch,sh,ph,* etc.)
single vowels — short sound first, then long diphthongs (e.g. *oy, ow*)
phonetic generalizations

Russell:

Ear training suggestions:
listening to rhymes
similarities in beginnings of names such as *Tom* and *Tina*
judging sounds for pitch and distance

Schell & Burns:

Use PPAR cycle: one principle or element is *presented, practised, applied,* and *reviewed* at a time.
Select words that contain specific sound elements and have children practise pronunciations.
List words that introduce newly learned skills.
Use games, filmstrips, transparencies, audio-tapes and recordings.

Tinker and McCullough:

Guide formulation of generalizations in child's own words and note exceptions to those phonetic generalizations.
Teach phonetic families derived from sight words already in child's vocabulary.
Teach discrimination of likenesses and differences in words.

Exercises:
Underlining like elements in lists of words, matching words that begin alike, or end alike; matching or underlining words that rhyme; substituting initial consonants or vowels.
Teach phonograms.
Teach syllabication.

Deficient phonic knowledge:
1) pronounce names;
2) comment on written letter (tall *L*) (six *J*'s in class).

Zintz:

Reteaching of any phonetic element missed should be planned for those who need it. Exercises that will provide needed practice can be found in many teachers' manuals or children's workbooks.

Children must learn all the skills in word perception so that they will be able to pronounce words readily in their reading. Phonetic analysis will help in word perception.

Phonetic skills to be taught include:

1) Single consonant letters — sound, not name;
2) Consonant blends.

To develop awareness of checking the sounding with the meaning of the sentence try the sound that fits the word needed in a particular context.

Instructional Materials (Commercial)

When individual pupils or groups of pupils are deficient in auditory analysis skills, corrective practice can be provided by using available commercial material such as:

1 *Clifton Audio/Visual Reading Programme* (ESA): This instructional programme consists of forty cards (297cm x 210cm) which introduce most of the more common phonic elements in English, from single letter sounds to prefixes and suffixes. These cards are accompanied by tapes and a workbook. (For use with individual pupils or small groups using head sets and a junction box fixed to the tape recorder.)

2 *Consonant-Vowel Blend Matching Cards* (Philip & Tacey): Two boxes contain picture-word cards which are cut into two pieces, through the word after the vowel, for instance, wi-ng. When the picture is put together so is the word.

3 *Creative Learning Pictures for Sounds* (ESA): Each large display picture is based on a different letter of the alphabet. Incorporated in the picture are many names, colours and objects beginning with the letter for children to identify. (For use with groups of children or the whole class.)

4 *Dog House Game* (Better Books): A phonic game consisting of thirty-five phonograms along with eighty-four assorted consonants and consonant blends with which to build words. (For use with two or more children, potentially self-directive.)

5 *Family Pairs/More Family Pairs* (Hart Davis): These forty-eight picture-word cards can be used to play rummy or happy families, as initial consonant clusters are collected together in pairs. (For three, four or five players.)

6 *Fish Game* (Good Reading): The circular base board has eight initial consonant digraphs printed on it, and a fish pinned at the centre. The fish is spun and points to one of the digraphs. The sixteen cards, picture uppermost, are displayed and the correct one has to be chosen to match the digraph. The word appears on the back of the picture card for checking. (For use with individual children or small groups.)

7 *Initial Blends* (Galt): The cards in this set make use of pictures which match with initial consonant letter blends. These cards are self-corrective.

8 *I Spy* (Hart Davis): Picture-letter cards provide the stimulus for this well-known game, as children are invited to listen for other words which begin in the same way. (For use with small groups of children.)

9 *Junior Phonic Rummy* (Better Books): This game employs one hundred and ten of the most frequently occurring short vowel words from the most widely used Infant School basic reading books. A key picture is provided for each of the short vowel sounds. (For use with two or more children, potentially self-corrective.)

10 *Linguistic Block Series* (Scott Foresman): Rolling phonics, consonants; consists of a set of ten blocks involving eleven one-syllable words beginning with vowels and twelve consonant or consonant blends. Over eighty-five words can be built. (For use with individual children, children working in pairs, or a small group of children.)

11 *Listening to Sounds* (E.J. Arnold): This series consists of two workbooks which are accompanied by tapes. The preparatory work is with sound patterns leading on to letter sounds. Lotto games and Dominoes are also provided.

12 *Look, I'm Reading* (ESA): Envelopes: each letter of the alphabet and some digraphs are printed on separate envelopes which contain cards, words, and pictures which go with the letter.

13 *Make It* (Hart Davis): Each of these forty-eight cards has a letter printed on it. They can be used as a patience game to build three-letter words.

14 *Pair-It* (Hart Davis): The forty-eight cards in this pack represent the beginnings and ends of twenty-four words. Rummy can be played to collect the pairs that go together to make the word for the picture in each case. (For two, three, or four players.)

15 *Phonetic Word Drill Cards* (Better Books): These instructional materials involve three sets of cards. Each set has ten chart cards showing a different word ending on each side. Thus, there are two families of words on each basic chart card, or twenty families per set. Initial sound cards are suspended by plastic rings from the top of each basic chart card and are in line with the word endings. As each card is flipped, a new word appears and then the chart can be reversed and the operation repeated. With these three sets eight hundred and sixty-four words can be formed. Sixty common word endings are involved. (For use with individual children, children working in pairs, or with a group of children under proper direction.)

16 *Phonic Alphabet Activity Cards* (Philip & Tacey): A set of twenty-four alphabet cards with one letter on each card, three words and pictures. The main picture on each card is also a cut-out shape for easy reproduction by the child

17 *Phonic Crosswords* (Good Reading): These fifty crosswords offer children practice in writing down fairly common words, with each crossword emphasizing one particular sound or group of sounds. Sequencing the letters is linked with the meaning of the word answer to the clue.

18 *Phonic Footsteps. Stages 1 and 2* (Good Reading): These games are played with coloured counters and the players are required to identify the middle of each word. Stage 1 — short vowels. Stage 2 — vowel digraphs. (For children working in pairs.)

19 *Phonic Rummy (Four Sets)* (Better Books): These games are designed to teach short vowels and vowel principles. Each set contains two packs of sixty cards presenting words suitable for the age levels masked on each set. (For use with two to four children, potentially self-directive.)

20 *Phonic Self-Teacher* (Galt): This boxed apparatus consists of a set of seven base-boards with four letters on each, and fifty-six picture cards with the appropriate initial letter on the reverse. The pictures are sorted into their letters and checked.

21 *Rabbit Game Parts 1 and 2* (Good Reading): Picture-word cards and two initial letter wheels give self-checking material for pupils to practise twenty-four initial letters with their appropriate picture names. (For a group of four children.)

22 *Reading Laboratory/Word Games* (Science Research Associates): This box contains five of each of forty-one different games. The games cover various phonic and structural skills. (To be played between pairs of pupils.)

23 *Rhyming Pairs* (Galt): Picture cues are provided to help the child to match words which rhyme. The pairs of cards are also cut in such a way as to provide a self-check. (For individual children or small groups of children.)

24 *School House* (Science Research Associates): This word attack skills pack contains two of each of one hundred and seventy cards in ten units. Each card develops a particular phonic unit from rhyming words to affixes.

25 *Sort and Sound Word Making Cards/Sort and Sound Vowel Digraph Cards* (Philip & Tacey): This boxed apparatus consists of picture-word cards which are cut through at the letter-sound boundaries. As the picture is reconstructed, so is the word in each case.

26 *Sound Links* (Galt): Three boxes each containing three sets each of four cards (twenty-four cards in each box), enable the child to identify initial and final letters of words. The cards have pictures and cuts which act as self-checking devices.

27 *Stott Games* (Homes McDougall): Consists of twenty-nine items arranged in a variety of games and activities. Gives extensive practice in phonic attack skills and leads to words in context. (For use with individual children, or children working in pairs or small groups.)

28 *Sussex Vowel Sorting and Word Cards* (Philip & Tacey): The box containing the cards is sub-divided into two rows of five recesses, two for each short vowel. The child is required to sort the picture-word cards into each recess according to the vowel in the picture-word card set.

29 *Take One Stage 1* (Good Reading): A patience game, matching picture cards with their initial consonant digraphs. (For individual children.)

30 *Turn the Wheel* (Good Reading): The base board has squares for picture-word cards, a wheel attached at the centre, and twelve initial consonant digraphs printed around the edge. When spun, the wheel will stop at positions which invite each of four players to choose one of his six cards (the one which goes with the selected digraph) and place it in his 'home' square. The first player to get all his cards 'home' is the winner. (For a group of four children.)

31 *Vowel Sounds Snap Game* (Philip & Tacey): This traditional snap game can be used for choosing rhyming words. Each of six boxes contains sixty playing cards. There is one box for each short vowel and a sixth box introduces an assortment of all five short vowels.

32 *Word Blends* (Better Books): A set of subdivided, folding cards that highlight consonant blends and digraphs. A total of one hundred and forty-four words are formed. (For use with individual children, children working in pairs or a small group of children.)

33 *Word Maker* (Galt): This apparatus uses rhyming words to teach basic word patterns. Boxes 1 and 3: letter words, Box 3: final *e* and final consonant clusters. The pictures make this material self-checking.

34 *Word Slides* (Longman): Seventy-two different cards, twelve at each of six levels of phonic difficulty, give the child opportunities to decide which grapheme completes each word. These cards are self-correcting. (For use with individual children.)

Instructional Materials (Teacher/Pupil Constructed)

When individual pupils or groups of pupils are deficient in auditory analysis skills, corrective practice can be provided by using teacher- or pupil-made materials such as the following:

1 *Authors with Beginnings:* Words are printed on corners of cards — four cards to a set. A set consists of four words that begin with the same consonant blend. This can be highlighted by underlining the first two letters or writing them in red. Each child is dealt four cards and one child begins the game by calling for a word beginning with a given blend. If he gets the word he may continue to call for words. When his opponent indicates that he does not have the blend called for, the child draws from the deck of cards that is face down on the table. The child who acquires the most sets wins. (For use with two to four children, potentially self-directive.)

2 *Baseball:* A baseball diamond is drawn on the blackboard or on cardboard. Two groups of children are chosen. The pitcher flashes a blend. If the batter calls a word beginning with the blend, he has made a hit and moves to first base.

Should the next batter score a hit also, he moves to first base and the previous batter advances to second. Soon the runs begin to come in. Teams change sides just as soon as three outs (wrong answers) have been given. The team with the most 'runs' wins. (For use with groups of children.)

3 *Blend Fishing:* Consonant blend cards are cut in the shape of fish. A paper clip is slipped over each card. Fishermen are equipped with fish hook (small magnet). Each child takes a turn trying to catch a fish. If he can call a word that begins with the consonant blend sound on the fish he has caught, he may keep the fish. If he is unable to think of a suitable word, he returns the fish, face down, to the fishpond. (For use with two children or a group of children, potentially self-directive.)

4 *Clothespeg Wheel:* Cut out a circular piece of cardboard about 30cm in diameter. Paste or draw pictures of common objects around the periphery of the board. Equip the child with a box of clothespegs on each of which is printed a consonant blend. He then matches the clothespegs with the proper pictures. For example, the *fr* clothespeg would be placed over the picture of a *frog;* the *pl* clothespeg over the picture of a *plum*. For use with individual children, potentially self-directive.)

5 *Deezio:* A set of twenty-five cards is constructed. Recommended card size is 6cm x 8cm. An initial blend is written in two diagonal corners. A word beginning with this initial blend is written in the centre of the card. It is necessary to have at least two cards with the same initial blend, but the word in the centre should differ. The twenty-fifth card will have no duplicate. This card has a drawing of a funny face and is 'Deezio'.

All cards are dealt to the players and each player immediately looks for pairs of cards with the same blends. He places these pairs in front of him, saying the word on each card as he puts them down. If he cannot read the words, another player may tell him, but he must hold the pair until his next turn. Then the player to the left of the person with the most cards begins playing by drawing a card. He draws a card from the player holding the most cards. The

drawer attempts to match the card with one in his hand. If he has a pair, he places them in front of him and reads the words. If no match is made, he retains the card in his hand. The playing continues clockwise around the table. The player who matches all his cards first wins. The rest continue to play until one person is left with 'Deezio'; he is the 'Deezio'. (For use with three to five children, potentially self-directive.) (This game and the games *Happy Ending* and *Word Flight* were devised by Hildegard Ziegler et al; teachers at the Madison, Wisconsin Public Schools.)

6 *Finding Partners:* Two types of cards are placed in an envelope, some involving word endings and others consonant blends. The cards are distributed to a group of children. Those children receiving cards with blends move around among the children to see if they can form a word by combining their cards. When a word has been formed the child says, 'We made _____ with our cards.' Since there is the possibility that other blends may fit the ending, the teacher asks if anyone else can help make a word. The process continues until all pairing is exhausted. (For use with a group of children.)

7 *Go Fish:* This is a game, similar to 'Old Maid', designed to teach the sounds of initial consonants. Children select cards from each other or from the pack in an attempt to make a pair. (For use with two to four children, potentially self-directive.)

8 *Lotto Blends:* With the help of the children, the teacher prepares cardboard master cards 20cm x 28cm in size. These master cards are blocked off vertically and horizontally into twenty-five small squares. The middle space is marked *free*. Individual consonant blends are placed on the twenty-four spaces that remain. Each master card must have the same blends on it but in different positions, twenty-four words known by the children on sight that begin with the consonant blends are placed in the envelope. As individual words are drawn from the envelope and called, the players find the consonant blends on their master cards and cover them with a marker. The marker may be a kernel of corn, a bean or a small piece of

cardboard. The first child to cover a row of consonant blends in a straight line, vertically, horizontally or diagonally, calls out 'lotto'. If he has not erred, he is declared the winner. (For use with a group of children, potentially self-directive.)

9 *Pockets:* Obtain some cheap envelopes and mount them on a chart as pockets for 8cm x 13cm cards. A consonant blend is printed on each envelope. The cards have pictures or drawings on them which are to be placed in the pockets beginning with the appropriate consonant blend. By using an identification scheme on the backs of the cards, this activity can be made self-corrective. (For use with individual children, potentially self-directive.)

10 *Sound Box:* Choose a cardboard box with subdivisions — one that has been used to package bottles is ideal. By using common pins, label each subdivision with a small card on which a blend has been written. Players draw picture cards from a pile and attempt to place them in the space labelled with letters that represent the beginning blend sounds of the words pictured. Points can be given for correct choices. This activity can be made self-corrective by printing the correct letters on the backs of the picture cards. (For use with one or more children, potentially self-directive.)

11 *Spin and Call:* Divide a large cardboard circle into eight sections. Attach a large pointer to the centre of the circle so it spins freely. The player spins the pointer and calls a word beginning with the particular consonant blend to which it points when coming to a stop. If a correct word is called, he scores one point. A record should be kept of words called so no repetitions take place. (For use with two children or a group of children.)

12 *What Am I?:* On individual cards write riddles which give initial consonant blends as clues. For example, 'I grow in bunches on trees. I am good to eat. I begin with a *gr* sound. What am I?' Each child in the group has a chance at a riddle card. If he guesses the answer he is given the card. The child with the largest number of cards is the winner. By placing the answers on the backs of the cards, this activity can be made self-corrective. (For use with a group of children, potentially self-directive.)

Problem **4 Inability to Use
Context Clues**

4 Inability to Use Context Clues

The child is unable to use meaning suggested by the story or sentence to anticipate new or unfamiliar words.
The ineffective use of context clues forces the child to analyse carefully many words that should be identified with a minimum inspection. This slows down his reading.

Possible Causes
1 Lack of training in using clues.
2 Word-by-word reading; limited vocabulary.
3 Carelessness in word recognition.
4 Teacher does not make use of contextual instruction.
5 Mental immaturity.
6 Lack of experience.
7 Material too difficult.
8 Lack of motivation.
9 Lack of phonic ability.

Signs of Disability
1 Gives word that does not fit context and does not see that it is an error.
2 Unusual difficulty in recognzing words specifically related to a topic.
3 Weakness in citing words expected in a passage about a certain topic.
4 Makes as many errors in reading words in context as when reading a list of words.
5 Refusal to hazard a guess at a word when its meaning is clearly indicated by the rest of sentence.
6 Unsatisfactory comprehension.

Remedial Work
1 The teacher should place greater emphasis upon the readiness development which precedes the reading of a topic. The study of pictorial aids (tables, charts, graphs, pictures), the planning and development of the background and introduction to new words, are forms of building expectancy clues.
2 Meaningful reading rather than just recall should be emphasized.
3 Teachers' manuals contain many suggestions for the introduction and building of readiness. Suggestions of methods from a good manual may be applied to other reading material.
4 Remedial training should be based upon having the child read materials that are so easy that he encounters about one new word in every forty running words.
5 In the more severe cases, a separate problem may be stated for each paragraph or sentence.
6 The child should use the context plus the initial sound to help him solve his word recognition problems.
7 Riddles and puzzles are excellent for practising the use of context clues.

Sample Exercises:

1 Present sentences in which words are missing. The pupils are instructed to read the sentences and decide which word(s) fit the blanks most appropriately.

Examples: They put the _____ in the bank.
      paper   letter   money

The day was bright and _____.
sunny   dark   cloudy

Bill had to _____ if he should _____ the fort against attack.
defend   decide

2 Present sentences in which a phonic clue is given to aid the pupil in providing missing words. Pupils are instructed to think of words which fit the blanks most appropriately.

Examples:
Betty said she would r____ the ball on the floor.
The cat dr____ the milk.
He was going to ____ow his shoe at the barking dog.

3 Use a modified cloze technique.
Select a group of sentences from reading materials and delete several letters in key words, or key words themselves. On the basis of context the children are to attempt to identify the words with missing letters, or the missing words. (Ruddell)

The p_____ drew their covered wagons into a large _____ for protection at night.
The huge truck crashed th_____ the wall and _____ the building.
The s_____ caught the wind and the crew cheered as the _____ sped _____ the finish line.

Teaching Suggestions

The following suggestions are drawn from the work of reading specialists. Sources are listed under the authors' names in the bibliography.

Betts:

Pupils must have materials that are not only within their experience and interest, but also rich enough in concept to be challenging. Repetition in meaningful situations results in retention.
Context clues:
Develop habit of verifying conclusions reached through other word recognition techniques by criterion, 'Does this make sense?'
Develop habit of examining context, sentences, paragraphs or whole selection, for clues to recognition and meaning.
Develop ability to use typographical aids, quotation marks, italics, boldface type, parentheses, footnotes.
Develop ability to use language structure aids.
Develop ability to interpret figures of speech.
Develop ability to recognize inter-relatedness of context clues and versatility in using them.
Develop ability to use pictorial representations.

Bond and Tinker:

Place greater emphasis on readiness development which precedes reading of a topic: introduction of unit or selection; picture study prior to reading; vocabulary development; planning of expected outcomes.
Meaningful reading rather than just recall.
Exercises using pictures to build expectancy clues; knowledge of topic.
Use materials with low level of difficulty.
Exercises in which meaning of sentence indicates word to be recognized; missing words are filled in using initial elements given; context plus initial elements aid word recognition.
Riddles in which context gives the answer.

Durrell:

Present words in sentences and pause before unknown word; child says word.

Harris:

Child looks at illustration, thinks of what the sentence means, and attempts to guess at missing word or word not in sight vocabulary.

Child uses a combination of phonics, structural analysis and context clues.

Heilman:

Stress importance of keeping the mind on what has been read and how the present sentence (being read) builds on this meaning. If context is not enough, glance through the word to detect a prefix, the root word, or an inflectional ending. When no prefix is found, the first syllable is isolated to unlock the word and the reader may have to work further through the word. If the word is not solved by this attack, the reader may go on past the word for additional clues. This step may call for re-reading the sentence.

Kottmeyer:

Give short paragraphs in which key words are omitted. Be sure that only one word will fit each blank.

Encourage child to guess word. This centres attention on meaning.

In case of extreme reading disability, use easier material.

Money:

Use sentences which contain words that add thought to the sentence.

For example:

When Jane wants to go fast, she must *run*.

As opposed to:

Run, Jane, run.

Use picture clues to gain knowledge of a topic.

Strang, McCullough and Traxler:

Teach the pupils to be aware of the following types of context clues:

1 *Direct explanation* of the word is given in the sentence.
2 *Experiential* — the meaning of the word is given by something that the pupil has experienced.
3 *Comparison and contrast* — the unknown word is used in direct contrast to a known word.
4 *Synonym or restatement* of the word gives the meaning.
5 *Familiar expression or language experience.*
6 *Summary* — the unknown word summarizes part of the content.
7 *Reflection of a mood or situation* which has already been described.

Ruddell:

Teach child to use the following information in attempting to identify an unknown word:

picture content

word and sentence meaning

word order in a sentence

meaning derived from previous content material

Children should be taught to question the choice of a word suggested by the context.

For example:

Does the word suggested 'match' the grapho — phonic characteristics of the word in print?

Does the word 'fit in' with the illustration?

Does the word make sense in the story?

Does the word fit the word-order of the sentence?

Russell:

Needs development under (professional) teacher guidance. Use context clues in lower grades as an attack on words in response to teacher suggestion rather than putting emphasis on technical names of context clues.

Aids in context clues are often too technical for systematic use in elementary school.

Recommend use of context clues in combination with word analysis activities.

Tinker and McCullough:

Encourage the imaginative interpretation of pictures accompanying a story.

Direct attention to contextual meanings.

Encourage the 'guessing' of a word that makes sense.

Wilson:

Child may not be aware of contextual clues.

Teach child anticipation if he is aware of contextual clues and does not use them.

By substituting initial consonant of an underlined word in sentence, make the sentence make sense.

Emphasize importance of checking to see that identified word makes sense in sentence.

Ask children to fill blanks in sentence to make sense.

Stress use of meaning clues to check visual clues.

Use dictionary meanings to fit context.

Instructional Materials (Teacher/Pupil Constructed)

When individual pupils or groups of pupils are deficient in the use of context clues, corrective practice can be provided by using the following types of activities.

(N.B. Many of the instructional materials described in the previous chapters will be suitable here.)

1 Activities in which context clues plus initial elements are used as aids to word recognition.

He will get some apples at the sh _____ .

shop   shore   farm

2 Activities using pictures to build expectancy clues.

a) Look at the picture above. In it you will see some animals doing funny things. Then look at the sentence below. Draw a line around the name of the animal that the sentence is about.

He is opening his mouth for a peanut.

elephant   hippopotamus   monkey

b) Study the picture illustrating a selection prior to reading it. The unit to be read may deal with various types of animals in the zoo. A study of the picture would enable the children to anticipate the names of the animals. Then before each selection is read, a review of the names of the animals in the selection can be made. The picture clues become a great aid to recognition of such difficult words as baboon, kangaroo, hippopotamus, elephant, zebra, and crocodile.

3 Activities using knowledge of the topic to build expectancy clues.

a) Mark the words you would expect to read about in a farm story, *F*. Mark those in a city story, *C*.

shops   cattle   tractor   street
chickens   escalator   traffic
crowds   haystack   barn   meadow

b) Which of the following phrases would you expect an old seafaring man to use. Put *S*, before them.

_____   a square-rigged ship
_____   pretty autumn leaves
_____   over the bulwarks
_____   a modern tractor

4 Print several sentences on coloured card and then cut each sentence into two pieces. Ask the children to place the two correct pieces back together, (Can be used with individual pupils or with small groups.)

Tania likes   to the movies.
Lance built   her breakfast.
Gloria went   his tree house.
Diana ate   her new dolls house.

5 Select several sentences from the children's reading material. Delete a key word in the sentence and leave a black space. Provide the key word with another word in a multiple choice item. Based on the context the children are to circle the appropriate word. (Ruddell)

Herb's _____ is to clean out the garage.

responsibility   respectability

Peg lost her footing and fell _____ into the water.

backward   upward

The _____ told the boys where to find the racing book.

librarian   politician

6 Present sentences which contain unusual words whose meaning can be arrived at by using contextual clues. Pupils are instructed to read the sentences carefully before deciding on an answer.

Examples:

John will *deflate* the tyre by opening the valve.

Deflate means (1) put air in (2) let air out of (3) turn over (4) damage

The edifice on the corner of the street is a library.

Edifice means (1) bicycle (2) train (3) building (4) ship

The old trunk was *capacious* enough to hold all John's clothes.

Capacious means (1) unclean (2) colourful (3) small (4) large

7 Activities in which the meaning of the sentence indicates the word to be recognized.

The boy rode over the snow on it. What was it?

     sleigh   shop   peanut

8 Exercises in which the child reads a paragraph, filling in the missing words using the initial elements given. He does not need to write them but reads the sentences to himself. Comprehension questions can be asked.

Billy caught the ball.

Then he th_____ the ball to his father.

Father c_____ the ball too.

Billy and his father were pl_____ catch.

9 Riddles in which the context gives the answer.

It lives in a zoo.

It hops about.

It carries its baby in its pouch.

It is a _____.

     horse   crocodile   kangaroo

10 Teachers construct a 'crossword' type puzzle involving vocabulary from reading material being used by the pupils. Remind the pupils to read the clues carefully and to be certain that each word they choose has the same number of letters as there are boxes for the word. The first letter of each word should be inserted for pupils who have difficulty working puzzles.

11 Cut from magazines pictures that represent vocabulary of high frequency: form classes, such as nouns (eyes, people); verbs (jump, eat, drink); and adjectives (little, blue, yellow). Paste the pictures in a large circle on cardboard. Attach a card pointer in the centre of the circle with a paper rivet. Prepare a set of word cards with the words representing the pictures. Each player spins the pointer and notes the word represented by the picture. He then sorts through the word cards, locates the word that matches the picture, and uses the word in a sentence.

12 Use illustration or large pictures that represent a variety of high frequency words for development. Prepare sentences on strips of card to match the action in the picture.

Example:

The boy threw the ball.

It crashed through the window.

The angry man is talking to the boy.

Then cut the sentences apart and provide a deck of word cards for each sentence. Mix the cards out of order.

     boy   the   ball   the   threw

The child builds a sentence to represent the action in the picture.

13 Prepare a paper tachistoscope with words for rapid exposure. Two children may be teamed. One child flashes the word, the other child pronounces it, and then the first child uses it in a sentence. A game variation of this activity, known as 'Fishing', may be developed by preparing individual word cards and placing a paper clip on each. The word cards are placed in a container and the child is provided with a 'fishing pole' — a short stick with an attached string and magnet. The child 'fishes' a word out of the container and reads it within a few seconds. If the child has difficulty reading the word the card is turned over and the picture clue is used, but the 'fish' must be thrown back. A new word card is drawn from the container until the child is successful. This activity can be used with a small group of children. Each correctly pronounced word scores one point. (Ruddell)

Problem 5 Inadequate Comprehension Skills

5 Inadequate Comprehension Skills

Children must be able to gain meaning from what they read. The good reader must be able to 'process' print efficiently and apply the ideas and meaningful relationships to both convergent and divergent thinking.

Possible Causes

1 Lack of general reading ability.
2 Lack of training to gain meaning from print.
3 Reading too slow or too fast.
4 Material too difficult.
5 Lack of experiential background.
6 Too much attention given to decoding.
7 Poor questioning techniques being used.
8 Not interested in the material — lack of motivation and concentration.

Signs of Disability

1 Unable to answer factual questions based on the material read.
2 Unable to find main idea of passage.
3 Unable to follow directions in print.
4 Unable to follow the sequence of events in material.
5 Unable to reproduce much of what was read.
6 Unable to construct an outline of the content.
7 Unable to answer anything but literal type questions in later primary years.
8 Unable to form judgements on what was read.

Remedial Work

1 Use materials that the child will be interested in, able to read and understand.
2 Ask a few simple questions at the literal level to begin with and then gradually increase the number and type of questions until the child is able to work with paragraphs and sequences of material.
3 Vary the assignment work so that the child will gain experience in solving a number of problems (e.g. written, puzzles, riddles, etc.)
4 Use short drills to teach specific skills such as finding the main idea or following directions.
5 Teach the child how to vary speed of reading without losing comprehension ability. Give short, speeded exercises and ask a few questions.
6 Read material to the pupil and develop listening comprehension skills to build confidence.
7 Use a variety of activities to encourage pupil response: art, drama, graphs etc.

Sample Exercises:

1 Ask a variety of questions which will probe understanding at the literal, non-literal (interpretive), critical, and creative levels.
   a) What did Tania find in the forest? (literal)
   b) What did Michael mean when he said that Diana had been 'sent on a wild goose chase'? (non-literal)
   c) Why did Michael telephone his mother? (interpretive)
   d) Were the police correct in arresting the beggar? (critical)
   e) What would you have done if you were in charge of the search party? (creative)

2 Use the cloze procedure to evaluate a pupil's understanding of reading material.
   Example:
   Lance saw smoke rising over the trees. He knew that it _____ not safe to build _____ fire in the forest.

3 Organize sentences into the correct order in a paragraph.
   Example:
   Place the following sentences in the correct order to make sense.
   a) The chickens looked under the hay.
   b) Finally, the brown hen saw some grain under the barn.
   c) In the yard, the brown hen looked for something to eat.
   d) She called to her chickens.
   e) They all had a good meal.

Teaching Suggestions

The following suggestions are drawn from the work of reading specialists. Sources are listed under the authors' names in the bibliography.

Bond and Tinker:

1 *Sentence Work.* Children must understand the vocabulary being used and the relationships involved. Children must be able to:

   a) read by 'thought units';
   b) understand punctuation usage;
   c) comprehend figurative language.

2 *Paragraphs and Selections.* Children must comprehend each sentence and the relationships between all language units in the reading passage.

Dechant:

Teach the pupil to develop a purpose for reading. Comprehension skills need to be practised in the following areas (depending on the maturity of the pupil):

1 Giving meaning to the phrase, clause, sentence, paragraph, and selection.
2 Understanding organization.
3 Locating main idea and supporting details.
4 Following directions.
5 Understanding relationships, figurative expressions.
6 Making inferences.
7 Recognizing and understanding aspects of characterization, style, purpose, etc. in literature.
8 Using ideas and integrating them with past experience.

Drummond and Wignell:

Children should be trained to gain the meaning from reading material as soon as possible. They should be given practice at three levels in material — literal, interpretive, and assimilative (critical) and should also be encouraged to be creative (appreciate their own ideas and feelings). The following comprehension skills should be taught:

1 Locate and understand the main idea: (suggest a title for a passage).
2 Select supportive details: (complete a sentence, draw a map or plan).
3 Understand directions or a sequence of events: (read recipes, directions for making a model, re-tell a story).

4 Understand organization of material: (teacher demonstrates use of index, table of contents, scanning techniques, simple report writing).

Gillespie and Johnson:

1 The 'directed reading lesson' is used with most readers. This technique involves:
   a) establishing a purpose for reading;
   b) directed reading and discussion;
   c) extending skills and abilities;
   d) enrichment and follow-up activities.

Teachers should be careful in their questioning techniques and should ensure that a variety of types of questions (factual, inferential, critical) are used.

2 The 'directed reading-thinking activity' (D—R—T—A) extends the directed reading lesson:
   a) identifying purposes for reading;
   b) guiding the adjustment of rate to purposes and material;
   c) observing the reading;
   d) developing comprehension;
   e) fundamental skill training activities: discussion, further reading, additional study, writing.

3 Basic skills in reading comprehension include: word, sentence, and paragraph meaning; organizational skills and critical reading skills.

Gilliland:

1 Use guided, part-by-part reading technique. Read the beginning of an exciting story to pupils, have them predict the outcome and then read to check their prediction.

2 Select materials that are of interest to the reader (pop lyrics, magazines, cartoons).

3 Use dramatization and art to illustrate the meaning of a passage.

4 Help pupils graph their progress.

5 Have reading sessions with no evaluation.

Ruddell:

Teach comprehension skills (details, sequence, cause and effect, main idea, predicting outcome, valuing, and problem solving) in each of three levels:
1 factual
2 interpretive
3 applicative

Instructional Materials (Commercial)

When individual pupils or groups of pupils are deficient in comprehension skills, corrective practice can be provided by using available commercial material such as:

1 *Action* (Scholastic Book Services): Useful for decoding and comprehension. A ninety-lesson reading programme including unit books, paperbacks of short stories and plays, posters and recorded readings.

2 *Breakthrough to Literacy* (Longman): A variety of instructional materials designed to train children to compose written language based on their spoken language. The materials include common vocabulary which is organized by the child through discussion and teacher involvement.

3 *Disco Pack* (Cassell): This pack of thirty-two work cards is based on Disco Books, which is a series of stories for older children (14-16 yrs) with R.A. 6+·

4 *Griffin Pirate Stories* (E.J. Arnold): Provide material suitable for readers from R.A. 6.0 up to remedial readers in secondary schools. Workbooks contain a variety of teaching materials and exercises to develop reading skills.

5 *Help!* (Nelson): Eighteen story books and six workbooks which are for older children with R.A.7 +. The workbook approach is informal throughout, with the accent on doing, making, acting and puzzling out.

6 *Language Centre 2* (Drake): This programme contains seventy different cards of graded reading difficulty with questions to answer (answers provided) and seventy different skill cards which provide for additional work.

These can all be marked by the children themselves. The programme includes listening-skills cassettes and language-development pictures, with books for children to log their own progress.

7   *One Two Three and Away* (Hart Davis): This beginning reading scheme is based on stories which develop through picture books, sentence books, sixteen main readers and three sets of six 'platform readers'. They are accompanied by workbooks and question cards which provide further reading practice and teach new skills.

8   *Reading Routes* (Longman): A boxed kit containing one hundred and forty-four folders with test and questions on one hundred and twenty topics. Answer cards are provided which suggest further work.

9   *Reading Workshops 6-10, 9-13* and *Remedial* (Ward Lock): These boxed materials present a structured, individualized approach to the development of comprehension, vocabulary and language skills in children who have already mastered basic reading techniques. They consist of workcards to be read, with questions to answer and answer cards for children to check their own work.

10   *Ready to Read* (Methuen): A wide variety of reading material which includes practice in understanding the meaning of pictures and print material. The programme aims to develop independent and thoughtful reading.

11   *S.R.A. Reading Laboratory* (Science Research Associates): A series of multi-level kits containing reading materials designed to develop the pupil's vocabulary, comprehension, and rate of reading.

12   *Thinklab 1* (Science Research Associates): A series of one hundred and twenty-five problems to be solved. Different types of problems are posed in writing, which challenge and motivate reluctant readers.

Instructional Materials (Teacher/Pupil Constructed)

When individual pupils or groups of pupils are deficient in comprehension skills, corrective practice can be provided by using the following materials and techniques:

1   *Choose the Best Title:* On Saturday, father took the children to the circus. They sat in the front row and saw the clowns, the elephants and the lions going by so close they could almost touch them. After the show was over in the big ring they had popcorn and a drink and walked around listening to the music. They saw the animals again in their cages.
(a)   Clowns, Elephants and Lions
(b)   A Good Day
(c)   A Day at the Circus

2   *Following Directions — Draw and Picture:* Draw a big house with two windows open and the door closed. Put a little barn beside the house. Put an orchard beside the barn. In front of the house draw a family made up of a mother, a father, two boys and a girl.

3   *Jumbled Sentences:* Disarrange sentences, direct pupils to put the parts in proper order.
Examples:
a)   in an accident / Jane thought / were injured / that the boys.
b)   is true / you read / don't believe / that everything.
Correctly arranged sentences can appear on the back of the exercise. (For use with individual pupils, potentially self-directive.)

4   *Making Sense:* Put the words in the right blank (cloze procedure).
walk   furry   difficult   children   scratch
One day the _____ were taking a _____ with their dog. They met a big black _____ cat. The cat tried to _____ the dog and the children had a _____ time.

5 *Missing Words:* Numbered sentences containing missing words are prepared. Pupils demonstrate comprehension of the sentences by choosing correct missing words.
Examples:
Many people have _____ for family pets.
Children learn many interesting things in _____.
_____ are those times during the year when people should relax and enjoy themselves.

a) dogs   b) holidays   c) schools

Correct answers can appear on the back of the exercise. (For use with individual pupils, potentially self-directive.)

6 *Omit Two:* Mount a picture on an individual card together with three sentences that tell something about the picture. Print two extra sentences that do not relate to the picture. Pupils are instructed to find the two irrelevant sentences. Correct answers can appear on the back of the exercise. (For use with individual pupils, potentially self-directive.)

7 *Pictures and Sentences:* Two or three pictures are mounted on individual cards together with fifteen or twenty sentences which have been printed on separate cards. Pupils are instructed to read each sentence and match it with the picture to which it refers. A marking scheme can be devised on the reverse side of the cards to make this activity self-corrective. (For use with individual pupils, potentially self-directive.)

8 *Pronoun Meaning:* Construct sentences containing the use of pronouns. Ask children to identify the person that the stressed pronoun refers to.
Example:
Mother took Tania and Diana to school. After *she* left they played with the other children.

Tania   Mother   Diana

9 *Punctuate Me:* Type paragraphs in which all full stops and capital letters have been omitted. Pupils are directed to designate the beginnings and endings of sentences by employing proper punctuation and capitalization. The correctly written paragraphs can appear on the back of the exercise. (For use with individual pupils, potentially self-directive.)

10 *Sentence Detective:* Give clues which refer pupils to a picture appearing in a story previously read. Ask them to find the sources of these clues on the page or in the picture. Correct sentences can appear on the back of the exercise. (For use with individual pupils, potentially self-directive.)

11 *Sentence Match:* Four sentences are prepared. Two of the four say approximately the same thing. Pupils are directed to find the synonymous sentences.
Examples:
The man went on and on until he became very tired.
The man wandered about until he found what he was looking for.
The man entered the wilderness looking for a place to build a cabin.
The man continued walking for a great distance until he was exhausted.

Correct answers can appear on the back of the exercise. (For use with individual pupils, potentially self-directive.)

12 *Split Sentences:* Pupils are given two envelopes. One envelope contains cards with sentence beginnings and the other with sentence endings. Pupils are directed to match suitable parts to form sentences.
Examples:
Jack and Jill went up the hill
I ran and ran until I was
As the sun began to rise it became

a) lighter and warmer   b) out of breath
c) to fetch a pail of water

Correct answers can appear on the back of the exercise. (For use with individual pupils, potentially self-directive.)

13 *Take Out the Extra Sentence:*
Come and see this.
Come for a ride.
'Please come here, mother', said Tom.
Look at the fish.
Some are big and some are little.

14 *True or False:* True and false statements that may or may not be related to the reading lesson can be used to help develop sentence comprehension. Since many such statements are humorous, children enjoy these exercises immensely.

Examples:

A 12-year old boy can run 100 miles an hour.

This sentence has more than seven words in it.

A wild tiger would make a fine house pet.

Correct answers can appear on the back of the exercise. (For use with individual pupils, potentially self-directive.)

15 *When, What, Where?:* Sentences which tell when, what or where are prepared. Pupils read each sentence and categorize it according to these designations.

Examples:

The Jones family spent their summer in the country.

A slender piece of metal that is driven into two blocks of wood can hold them together.

He said the world would come to an end last week.

Correct answers can appear on the back of the exercise. (For use with individual pupils, potentially self-directive.)

16 *Where's the Joker?:* Numbered sentences pertaining to a given subject are presented together with a sentence that does not belong. Pupils are directed to find the foreign sentence.

Examples:

The car is a Ford.

The body is red and the wheels are black.

The sky became dark and cloudy.

The top speed is 100 miles an hour.

Correct answers can appear on the back of the exercise. (For use with individual pupils, potentially self-directive.)

6 Inefficient Rates of Reading

Children need practice and guidance to develop flexibility in their reading rates. Some reading tasks require slow, careful reading while other reading materials can be treated with a much faster process involving skimming and scanning for relevant information.

Possible Causes

1 Defective vision.
2 Narrow perceptual span.
3 Improper eye movements.
4 Emotional instability.
5 Material uninteresting or too difficult.
6 Small sight vocabulary.
7 Difficulties in word recognition.
8 Over-analysis in word identification.
9 Insufficient use of context clues.
10 Lack of phrasing.
11 Vocalization.
12 Use of crutches such as finger or pointer.
13 Deficiency in word understanding and comprehension.

Signs of Disability

1 Uses same rate for all types of reading.
2 Slow, plodding, word-by-word reading.
3 Vocalization and lip movement.
4 Poor comprehension.

5 Hesitancy.
6 Poor eye movement.
7 Short memory span.
8 Reads too fast and sacrifices understanding.
9 Reads too slowly but comprehends well.
10 Omissions and substitutions.
11 Finger pointing and head movement.

Remedial Work

1 Don't sacrifice comprehension or fluency for increased rate. Aim to develop a rate of reading with good comprehension (70% or better) that does not let the child waste time.

2 Train the child to adapt the rate of reading to suit the type of material being read. The average reader may use four different rates of reading:
   a) analytical reading for study purposes;
   b) recreational reading of novels, newspapers, etc.;
   c) accelerated reading involving, specialized techniques such as previewing or surveying material;
   d) selective reading for specific information through the use of skimming and scanning.

3 Give the child practice in reading at various rates and ensure that comprehension level remains high. Gradually increase the rate until a 'ceiling' is reached. Use easy material to begin with.

4 Make certain that the reading materials are at the child's reading level and attempt to use materials that the child is interested in reading.

Sample Exercises:

1 Read quickly to find the main idea in the following paragraph:
We visited the zoo last Saturday. When we arrived we had lunch and later we saw the monkeys and some elephants.

2 Which word in the following list is different from the rest?
blue   yellow   green   dollar   red   pink

3 Find the main sub-headings in a chapter of your social studies book.

4 Locate the address of the local police station in the telephone book as quickly as you can.

5 Read the selection you have been given and answer the comprehension questions on the last page of your material.

Teaching Suggestions

The following suggestions are drawn from the work of reading specialists. Sources are listed under the authors' names in the bibliography.

Bond and Tinker:

1 Introduce new words in phrases.
2 Use material that is easy and avoids inane repetition and has a considerable amount of conversation.

3 Use dramatic readings, tape recordings, dummy or live microphone readings.
4 Encourage re-reading of selection to locate expressive phrases.
5 Have child prepare material to read orally.
6 Rapid exposure techniques of phrases.
7 Exercises: multiple choice in which choices are given in phrases; rapidly finding phrases to answer specific questions; marking off thought units in answer to questions; drawing line from phrase to word with similar meaning; locating phrases on certain page that appeal to different senses; reading sentences that have been separated into thought units.

Della-Piana:

Correctional Emphasis:
1 Word and phrase flash drills.
2 Phrase reading in context.
3 Use of line marker.
4 Word analysis study.
5 Give comprehension questions before reading sentences or larger units.
6 Practise reading with set for:
   a) recalling a sequence of events;
   b) specific details;
   c) causes of an event.
7 Vocabulary development.
8 Practise silent reading calling for frequent oral answers or following directions with motor responses.

Durrell:

1 First establish habits of accurate, attentive reading.
2 Give speed tests once or twice a week and record results on a graph for motivation.
3 Use gadgets for increasing speed reading; pacers, mechanical shutters, films, cardboard tachistoscopes.

Harris:

1 Primarily, eliminate specific interfering habits such as excessive word analysis, slow word recognition, word-by-word reading, lip movements and subvocal reading, finger pointing and head movement, improper eye movements.
2 Motivate a large amount of easy reading.
3 Give a series of timed silent reading exercises with comprehension checks.
4 Give practice in controlled reading and tachistoscopic training.
5 Present new words not in isolation but in phrases or sentences.
6 Use materials with few or no difficulties in word recognition and word meaning.
7 Provide a good model for imitation.
8 Provide practice on material in which phrases have been marked off.
9 Leave additional space between material typed or printed by hand.
10 Give unmarked selection to be marked off by phrases.
11 Give practice in recognizing phrases as units during brief exposure through:
   a) flash cards;
   b) tachistoscope — strip of stiff paper with opening the length of a full line moved down the page exposing one phrase at a time.

Heilman:

1 Improving slow rate of reading involves working with factors such as the reader's habits, skills and attitudes towards the material being read.
2 Provide practice in basic reading skills.
3 Provide practice in improving word-attack skills.
4 Teach to read in phrases, in logical thought units.

Money:

1 Use material with as many basic words as possible.
2 Use short sentences.
3 Watch the difficulty level of the concepts.

Tinker & McCullough:

1 Use material which offers no difficulty in recognition.
2 Direct attention to meaningful thought units and the aid provided by punctuation.
3 Demonstrate for imitation.
4 Separate reading material into phrases with short vertical lines.
5 Type materials with additional space between phrases.
6 Guide child to mark off phrase and then to do phrasing without marking or other artificial devices.
7 Provide incentives for reading faster. Use highly interesting material and stress pride in progress.
8 Use mechanical devices.

Zintz:

1 The best results are obtained when the material to be read orally is first read silently.
2 Good oral reading is developed by effective oral reading practice.
3 Easy, effective oral reading habits will require time to develop.
4 Probably too little time is given to teaching oral reading effectively.
   a) Reading of minutes.
   b) Substantiating a point of view.
   c) Reading reports.
   d) Choral reading.
5 The element of cruciality must not be overlooked. It is extremely important once in a while to read well orally.
6 Essential conditions for good audience reading:
   a) A real purpose for reading to others.
   b) A selection that is appropriate in type and difficulty.
      (1) Preliminary silent reading.
      (2) Attention to vocabulary difficulties.
      (3) Practice at reading orally before reading to a group.

Instructional Materials (Commercial)

When individual pupils or groups of pupils are deficient in reading rate, corrective practice can be individualized by using available commercial materials.

A Reading Machines

Dechant (1970) lists the equipment which is purported to help readers improve their rates of reading. The reading machines are grouped into tachistoscopes, accelerating devices and other reading related devices. Tachistoscopes are used to train a person's perceptual intake skills and are not considered very useful in teaching a person to read faster. Some of the more widely used reading accelerators and other instruments to improve reading rate are as follows:

1 *Controlled Reader* (EDL) distributed by Gateway Educational Media, Bristol: A ray of light from a central box moves down a page of print at a set rate of 800—1000 words per minute. This technique is intended to make the reader concentrate on the task and gradually improve in rate of reading.

2 *E.D.L. Skimmer* (EDL) distributed by Gateway Educational Material, Bristol: A ray of light from a central box moves down a page of print at a set rate of 800—100 words per minute. This technique is intended to make the reader concentrate on the task and gradually improve in rate of reading.

4 *S.R.A. Reading Accelerator* (Science Research Associates): A 'reading pacing device' which fits on top of a page of print and moves a shutter down the page at preselected speeds. There are three models available and the rate of reading can be increased from about 30 to over 300 words per minute.

B Reading Courses

There are numerous commercially prepared courses available which contain reading materials the publishers claim will help improve a reader's rate and flexibility of rate. Many of the courses merely present a sequence of articles with comprehension questions and urge the student to keep a record and attempt to read each article at a faster rate. Several reading programmes introduce practice in skimming and scanning skills, while others prepare special 'rate' cards for speed drill. A brief description of this latter type of course follows:

1 *Skimming and Scanning Text* (EDL) distributed by Gateway Educational Media, Bristol: This course contains material prepared for use with the *E.D.L. Skimmer* but which can also be used independently. The programme defines skimming and scanning in the following manner:

skimming — 'alternatively reading and glancing . . . your goal is to obtain an impression of the whole.'

scanning — 'looking just to find the information you want . . . a telephone number or a specific quotation in a book.'

2 *S.R.A. Reading Laboratory* (Science Research Associates): A series of kits containing reading cards, at various levels of difficulty, answer keys, record books, etc. A section of each kit is devoted to 'rate builders'. The reader usually completes three rate cards at a sitting, answers comprehension questions and records the scores on a progress chart.

3 *Reading Workshop 9-13* (Ward Lock): This material is designed for middle-school pupils. Practice in skimming and scanning (one hundred speed cards) is given as part of the instructional materials.

Instructional Materials (Teacher/Pupil Constructed)

When individual pupils or groups of pupils are deficient in word recognition skills, individualized practice can be provided by using teacher- or pupil-made materials such as the following:

1 Magazine articles that are fairly easy and interesting for the grade being taught are ideally suited for practice in improving rate of comprehension. It is suggested that expository articles 500—1000 words in length be mounted on cardboard. On the back side of the cardboard, ten questions pertaining to the article should appear. The answers to the questions should be written on a concealed slip of paper. A file of similar articles should be evolved so pupils can be given periodic practice in improving their comprehension rate. Each pupil is encouraged to keep his own progress chart and to try to improve his performance each time.

2 Provide pupils with 7cm x 12cm cards, show them how to expose a line of print very briefly by means of a quick raising and lowering of one card over the printed card. Encourage pupils to practise in this manner so they broaden their recognition span. (For use with individual pupils, potentially self-directive.)

3 Provide pupils with paragraphs in which they are instructed to underline key words. The selection with key words underlined can appear on the back of the exercise. (For use with individual pupils, potentially self-directive.)

4 Provide pupils with selections in which they are instructed to insert vertical lines between words to highlight the phrasing. The selection with lines inserted to show proper phrasing can appear on the back of the exercise. (For use with individual pupils, potentially self-firective.)

5 Give pupils a piece of cardboard 15cm square. Cut a portion of the top left-hand corner out, approximately 7cm wide and 3cm deep. Use this card to (a) practise phrase reading by exposing print in the cut-out portion; and (b) practise speed reading by placing the bottom of the card just above the first line of reading material and sliding the card down the page.

6 Prepare a passage of reading material with large spaces between phrases:
Example:
A monopoly   is a firm   which produces
the entire output   of an industry.

Have the pupils read the material as rapidly as possible and answer questions about the content or write a short summary.

7 Prepare a passage of material in newspaper format with the print in narrow columns. Have the pupils read rapidly down the column and answer comprehension questions about the content.

8 Provide pupils with paragraphs in which they are instructed to read rapidly and select a suitable title for each paragraph. Place a variety of titles under each paragraph and have the pupil select one. A variation of this exercise involves selecting the main idea or supporting facts.

9 Give pupils practice with reading materials which have had most of the structural words deleted. This will train the pupil to look for content words and gain the meaning of the passage. (Similar to 'telegraphic' writing.)
Example:
When Tania left _____ house, she went ____ _____ town _____ meet _____ mother.

10 Have the pupils pre-read the questions on a passage of material and then ask them to read the material and answer any questions they can. Train the pupils to check back very quickly into the reading material to find the answers to questions they have missed.

11 Teach pupils how to *preview* reading material.
Preview: look at any illustrations, read the title, the first paragraph, the first sentence of most of the other paragraphs, look at any other diagrams or pictures, and then read the last paragraph thoroughly. This technique does not take very long but it makes the reader concentrate, brings experiential background to bear, and provides the organizational framework and much of the content material in the passage. After previewing, the reader has time to read back over the material again.

N.B. Pupils should *only* be given reading rate work to correct specific inefficiencies in their reading performance. Reading rate should not be stressed when pupils have serious weaknesses in word skills or comprehension skills.

A Case Study

A Case Study

The preceding chapters have dealt with the identification and suggested treatment of specific reading problems. It was not the intention of this book to explain and analyse the complex and highly specialized skills needed to make a thorough diagnosis of a person with reading deficiencies. However, the use of a case study where most aspects of diagnosis and treatment are involved may well serve to clarify and coordinate the entire process.

The following discussion concerns Michael C, a boy of 13 years 8 months. Although Michael's case is only one of a vast number of reading disability cases, it is presented as a practical guide for the educator who is involved in attempting to help people overcome their reading problems. Many of the procedures discussed in this chapter were developed by Dr Jane Catterson at the University of British Columbia.

Case Study

1 Basic Data

Student's Name:	Michael C	*Parents:*	Mr & Mrs S. C
Date of Birth:	February 16, 1962	*Address:*	
Date of Test:	October 12, 1975		
Age at Testing:	13 years 8 months	*Telephone:*	
School:		*Name of Tester:*	
School Address:		*Location:*	
School Telephone:			

2 Background Information

Michael's mother accompanied him to the clinic and supplied the background information.

Michael has had all of his schooling at _____, and experienced difficulty in reading at the age of six when he was started on an ITA programme. At the age of nine, Michael began to receive assistance in reading and during the next three years, he worked with _____, the remedial reading teacher at the school. Michael has attended school regularly and has not presented any disciplinary problems to date.

Mrs C did not know whether Michael was still receiving remedial help in reading at the school. She mentioned that she had experienced difficulty with phonics as a child and that Michael's father was also weak in silent reading, citing as evidence her husband's habit of subvocalizing whenever he read the newspaper.

When he was nine, Michael was examined by an eye specialist and found to have no vision problems. His hearing was checked by the school nurse and was also satisfactory except for a slight hearing loss reported last year.

Mrs C commented that Michael was a nervous boy and that she was careful not to push him too hard in his work. She believes that Michael is discouraged about his lack of progress in reading but that he keeps his feelings to himself.

There is one other child in the family, a girl of eleven, who appears to be progressing quite well at school.

3 Test Given

A. *Durrell Analysis of Reading Difficulty:*

The Durrell Analysis is a standardized test that yields not only a composite score on oral and silent reading but provides an overview of areas of weakness. A careful administration of the test and study of its results makes an excellent basis for a remedial programme. The following sub-tests were used:

Oral Reading	In this test the child is asked to read paragraphs of gradually increasing difficulty until he makes seven errors, when the testing is discontinued. The child's score depends on both speed and comprehension.
Silent Reading	Testing is as above. The child is asked, however, to recount without help what he has read. No specific questions are asked.
Listening Comprehension	Since a child's ability to read depends on his comprehension of the spoken word, paragraphs of ascending difficulty are read to the child and questions asked afterwards. The child's ability to answer the questions gives a rough indication of his ability to learn to read.
Word Recognition	In this test the child is asked to identify orally common words flashed to him on a hand tachistoscope.
Word Analysis	If any words are missed above, the shutter is opened and the child is given the opportunity to sound out any words he has missed.
Visual Memory (P)	In the Primary level of this test, the child is asked to circle on a paper before him the words which are the same as the ones flashed to him on a hand tachistoscope.
Visual Memory (I)	In the Intermediate level of this test, the child is asked to write down what he can remember of words flashed to him on a hand tachistoscope.
Phonic Spelling	In this test a list of multi-syllable, phonetically spelled words is dictated to the child. Any phonetic spelling is accepted.
Spelling	A test of the ability to spell common words. Teacher dictates, child writes.

B. *Gates-McKillop Reading Diagnostic Test:*

Knowledge of Word Parts (V—I). In this sub-test an analysis is made of ability to identify and pronounce nonsense words, initial blends, and phonograms.

4 Results Obtained

A. Durrell

Oral Reading: Michael achieved a reading speed of *8½ years* with *fair to good* comprehension. His performance was marked by word-by-word reading, monotonous tone, poor enunciation, and a disregard for punctuation in several instances. Michael made elementary errors in all paragraphs and needed help in developing an adequate sight vocabulary with easy materials. Instructional level for oral reading would be equivalent to a reading age of 8 years.

Silent Reading: Michael found it impossible to perform at all in this aspect of reading. He either whispered or subvocalized even when told not to. His comprehension was not recorded at any level of the test.

Listening Comprehension: Only two levels were used *(Corresponding to reading ages of 8 and 9 years)* and Michael answered all questions correctly. It was obvious that Michael's reading difficulty did not rest on a lack of understanding of material read to him. The boy should be able to enjoy audio-visual materials of a much higher level than his reading tasks.

Word Recognition: Michael achieved reading-age level of *9 years* in this test of flashed words. He was adequate with single syllables and some two syllable sight words, but had difficulty with some blends ('cl' — said 'ch') and phonograms ('air' and 'ar'). Michael could not recognize on a flash words such as 'different', 'handle', and 'cleaned'.

Word Analysis: The reading-age level achieved in this test where Michael was asked to study and sound out words was also *9 years*. He was unable to analyse successfully: 'handle', 'cleaned', 'either' (Michael said 'over' — 'iver') and 'quarter' (he said 'quite'), even when given time to analyse.

Visual Memory of Words (Intermediate): When required to write a word from memory, Michael obviously found the task too difficult so the test was stopped, and the level dropped to the primary level.

Visual Memory of Words (Primary): Michael achieved a reading-age level of *8½ years* when he was asked to study a word for several seconds and then identify it from a number of words. In three out of the five errors he was wrong with the endings of words (added 's' twice, and 'al').

Phonic Spelling: Michael scored below the norms for this test. He had difficulty with *er* and used 'r' for this sound (Int*r*vent for int*er*vent, met*r* for met*er*). In fact he had a good deal of difficulty with vowel sounds and omitted them. This result reflects the word analysis tests results.

Spelling: The score in this test placed Michael at an age level of *9 years*. Most of the errors were caused by an attempt to spell phonetically ('payprs' for papers, 'brocan' for broken) emphasizing the boy's extremely weak sight vocabulary. Michael's handwriting was immature and mainly in printed forms.

B. Gates-McKillop

Knowledge of Word Parts: Michael had a score of 10 out of 23 nonsense words. In the blends aspect of the test Michael scored 20 out of 23 correctly, but his weakness with phonograms — particularly *(een, ew, ite, idge, able, ible)*, was clearly evident. Again, problems with vowels were evident.

5 Summary and Conclusions

Michael is functioning at a reading-age level of about *8 years* with the most marked weakness being in silent reading, where his level is probably no more than primary. His comprehension skills were fair to good (oral reading and listening). His handwriting was immature and uncontrolled.

6 Recommendations

Michael should begin instruction in reading at the reading-age level of *8 years* with high interest—low vocabulary materials and have practice in independent silent reading at the reading-age level of *7 years*.

A. Word Skills

1 Sight Vocabulary. Heavy emphasis on developing an adequate, functional, sight vocabulary starting at the reading-age level of *8 years*. Michael would benefit from the following types of exercises:
a) flash phrases
b) word sorting
c) substituting initial consonants and initial blends. (Stress the use of phonograms in the above.)

2 Word Analysis.
a) Auditory Analysis. Practise with hearing and identifying short and long vowel phonograms *(hit, book)*, and also some blends *(cl, qu, wr, str)*. Practise with hearing and counting the syllables in three syllable words *(car-pen-ter)*.
b) Visual Analysis. Drill to identify phonograms in words *(ade, een, ible, acle, idge)*.
c) Auditory/Visual. Practise with recognizing and blending common word parts using monosyllables: e.g. *blunt, drawn, stick*. Practise with easy polysyllabic words — *February, basketball*.

B. Comprehension Skills (Narrative)

Michael should be given comprehension exercises with materials at the reading-age level of *8 years*. His listening comprehension could be developed with materials from the reading-age levels of *8-9 years*. Oral questioning should continue to elicit main idea and details. Michael should also practise with cloze exercises where certain function or content words have been selectively omitted. In silent reading work, care should be taken to ensure that the level of the questions is not above that of the instructional material (particularly with teacher-made materials).

The importance of punctuation should be stressed and included as part of the work in sentences, paragraphs and selections. Certain passages could be presented without full stops and capital letters as an exercise.

Practice with sequencing in paragraphs and selections could involve a number of strips of material which have to be placed in the correct order. Further work of this nature involving organizational skills could deal with strips containing the main idea(s) and details of selections or chapters.

At all times it is important to ensure that the reading materials used by Michael are of a high level of interest and a low level of vocabulary difficulty.

7 Instructional Materials

In addition to the numerous materials and activities suggested in Chapters I to VI, a very good selection of instructional materials is given in *Reading: A Source Book for Teachers* (Drummond and Wignell, Heinemann Educational, 1979).

For the convenience of the teacher, a proposed lesson plan is presented in Appendix C. This arrangement allows for daily or weekly planning and can either take the form of the one worksheet or, alternatively, consist of separate worksheets for each of 'Word Skills', 'Sight Vocabulary', and 'Comprehension'.

Appendices

The 100 Most Frequent Words Edwards and Summers

the	as	not	may	each	up	no	because
of	or	can	there	two	such	must	see
and	with	your	has	about	then	water	like
a	on	they	I	should	time	also	much
to	this	we	other	what	its	first	people
in	by	his	some	than	would	very	called
is	was	will	more	been	how	good	place
that	he	if	were	into	number	him	through
it	from	an	had	them	made	same	work
are	have	when	their	use	out	could	new
for	at	all	used	make	most	who	small
you	which	but	many	do	only	any	over
be	one	these	so				

The 100 most frequent word types listed above, accounted for nearly 50% of the 250,000 word tokens used in the study. (Edwards, 1974.)

The Edwards List of 800 Easy Words

a	arm	beautiful	board	buy	clean	cut	ear
about	around	became	boat	buzz	climb		early
across	arrow	because	book	by	clock	dad	east
act	as	bed	both		close	dance	eat
add	ask	bedroom	bottom		clothes	dark	egg
aeroplane	asleep	bee	bow	cabbage	clown	day	else
afraid	at	been	bowl	cage	cluck	dear	elephant
after	ate	before	bow-wow	cake	coat	deep	end
afternoon	automobile	began	box	calf	cock-a-	did	engine
again	away	begin	boy	call	doodle-doo	dig	enough
ago		behind	branch	came	cold	dinner	even
air	baa	being	bread	can	colour	dish	ever
all	baby	believe	break	cap	come	do	every
almost	back	bell	breakfast	car	coming	does	everything
alone	bad	belong	bright	care	cook	dog	eye
along	bag	beside	bring	careful	cool	doll	
already	bake	best	brother	carry	corn	done	face
also	baker	better	brought	case	corner	don't	fall
always	ball	between	brown	cat	cost	door	family
am	balloon	big	bug	catch	could	down	far
an	band	bigger	build	caught	count	draw	farm
and	bang	bill	building	chair	country	dress	farmer
animal	bank	bird	bump	chick	cover	drink	fast
another	bark	birthday	bunny	chicken	cow	drive	fat
answer	barn	bit	burn	child	crab	drop	father
any	barnyard	black	bus	children	cried	drum	feather
anyone	basket	blew	bush	Christmas	cross	dry	feed
anything	bath	block	busy	circus	crumb	duck	feel
apple	be	blow	but	city	cry		feet
are	bear	blue	butter	clap	cup	each	fell

felt	gate	head	in	letter	milk	no	peanut
fence	gave	hear	inside	lie	milkman	noise	peep
few	get	heard	into	life	mill	north	pennies
field	gift	heat	is	light	mind	nose	penny
fill	girl	heavy	it	like	minute	not	people
find	give	held	its	line	miss	note	pet
fine	glad	hello		lion	Miss	nothing	pick
finish	go	help		listen	mix	now	picnic
fire	goat	hen	jar	little	money	nut	picture
first	God	her	job	live	monkey		pie
fish	going	here	joke	lock	moo	of	piece
fit	gold	herself	jump	log	moon	off	pig
five	gone	hid	just	lolly	more	often	pin
flag	good	hide		long	morning	oh	pink
flat	goodbye	high	keep	look	most	old	place
flew	got	hill	kept	lost	mother	on	plan
floor	grandfather	him	kill	lot	mouse	once	plant
flower	grandmother	himself	kind	loud	mouth	one	play
fly	grass	his	kitchen	love	move	only	please
follow	gray, grey	hit	kitten	lunch	Mr	open	pocket
food	great	hold	knew		Mrs	or	point
foot	green	hole	knock		much	orange	policeman
for	grew	home	know	made	mud	other	pond
found	ground	honey		mail	mum	our	pony
four	grow	hop		make	music	out	poor
fox	guess	horn	lady	man	must	outside	pop
free		horse	laid	many	my	over	post
fresh		hot	lake	march		own	present
friend	had	house	lamb	mark			press
frog	hair	how	land	matter	nail		pretty
from	hall	hungry	large	may	name	page	puff
front	hand	hunt	last	me	near	paint	pull
fruit	happen	hurry	late	meat	neck	pan	push
full	happy	hurt	laugh	meet	need	paper	put
fun	hard		lay	men	nest	park	puppy
funny	has		learn	meow	never	part	
	hat	I	leaves	met	new	party	
	have	ice	left	mice	next	pat	quick
	hay	if	leg	might	nice	paw	quiet
game	he	I'll	let	mile	night	pay	quite
garden			let's				

rabbit	same	sign	squirrel	talk	to	visit	who
race	sand	silk	stand	tall	today	voice	why
rain	sang	sing	star	tap	toe		wide
rake	sat	sister	start	teach	together	wagon	wild
ran	save	sit	station	teacher	told	wait	will
read	saw	six	stay	teeth	tomorrow	wake	win
ready	say	skate	step	tell	too	walk	wind
real	school	skin	stick	ten	took	want	window
red	sea	skip	still	tent	top	war	wing
rest	seat	sky	stone	than	town	warm	winter
rich	see	sled	stood	thank	toy	was	wish
ride	seed	sleep	stop	that	train	wash	with
right	seem	sleepy	store	the	tree	watch	without
ring	seen	slide	story	their	trick	water	woke
river	sell	slow	straight	them	tried	wave	wolf
road	send	small	street	then	trip	way	woman
roar	sent	smell	string	there	trunk	we	wonder
robin	set	smile	strong	these	try	wear	wood
rock	seven	smoke	such	they	turkey	wee	word
rode	shake	sniff	suit	thin	turn	weed	work
roll	shall	snow	summer	thing	turtle	week	world
roof	she	so	sun	think	two	well	worm
room	sheep	soft	sunshine	this		went	would
rooster	shell	sold	supper	those	umbrella	were	write
root	shine	some	sure	though	uncle	west	
rope	ship	something	surprise	thought	under	wet	yard
round	shoe	sometime	swam	three	until	what	year
row	shop	song	sweet	threw	up	wheat	yellow
rub	short	soon	swim	throw	upon	wheel	yes
run	should	sound	swing	ticket	us	when	you
	show	soup		tie	use	where	your
sad	shut	splash	table	tiger		which	
safe	sick	spot	tail	time	vegetable	while	zoo
said	side	spring	take	tired	very	white	

The 800 'easy' words were developed for a Primary Grades Readability Formula developed by the author.

Lesson Plan

WORD SKILLS				Child: *Michael, C*	
				Date:	
				Lesson: *1*	

General Target Skills	Special Target Skills	Content	Technique	Mode of Response	Comments
A. ANALYSIS					
1 Audio/Visual Integration.	*Short vowels*	*Words containing a,e,i,o,u, vowels.*	*Teacher pronounces word.*	*Child circles correct response.*	*10/10. No problem evident.*
2 Applied phonics.		*'Happy' words. Soft sounds. Garden tools.*	*Word sorting (classification exercise).*	*Written.*	*7/12. Too difficult.*
3 Visual discrimination/visual memory.	*Seeing phonograms.*	*ook, eak, ight.*	*Flash cards.*	*Oral and written.*	*Oral =8/8. Written=5/5.*
B. SIGHT VOCABULARY					
1 Words in context.	*Content words.*	*Passage of 300-400 words (reading age 8 years).*	*Flash cards.*	*Oral.*	*4/6.*
2 Special vocabulary.	*Edwards— Summers 100 words.*	*First fifty words.*	*Words on a sheet.*	*Written.*	*45/50.*

COMPREHENSION SKILLS

General Target Skills	Linguistic Unit	Sub-Skills	Content	Exercise Type	Mode of Response	Comments
1 *Improving instructional level.*	*a) Sentence.* *b) Selection.*	*Following sequence and details.*	*Passage of 300-400 words (reading age 8 years).*	*Guided silent reading.*	*Oral.*	*6/6.* *No problem.*
2 *Improving silent reading level.*	*Selection.*	*Following sequence and details.*	*Passage of 300-400 words (reading age 8 years).*	*Reading a longer selection*	*Silent reading — written.*	*7/10.*
3 *Listening comprehension.*	*Selection.*	*Listening for main ideas and details.*	*Short story (reading age 8 years).*	*Listening to selections.*	*Oral.*	*14/15. Very good response.*

Bibliography

Books

Aukerman, R. *Approaches to Beginning Reading*. Chichester, John Wiley & Sons Ltd, 1971.

Bateman, B. 'Three Approaches to Diagnosis and Educational Planning for Children with Learning Disabilities'. *Academic Therapy Quarterly,* II Summer 1967 (b).

Betts, Emmett A. *Foundations of Reading Instruction*. New York, American Book Company, 1946.

Bloomfield, L. & Bernhart, L. *Let's Read: A Linguistic Approach*. Detroit, Wayne State University Press, 1961.

Bond, G. & Tinker, M. *Reading Difficulties: Their Diagnosis and Correction*. New York, Appleton-Century-Crofts, 1967.

Bormuth, John R. (ed.) *Readability in 1968*. National Council of Teachers of English, 1968.

Buros, D. *Reading Tests and Reviews*. New Jersey, The Gryphon Press, 1968.

Chall, J. *Learning to Read: The Great Debate*. Maidenhead, McGraw-Hill Book Co (UK) Ltd, 1970.

Critchley, M. *Dyslexic Child*. London, William Heinemann Medical Books Ltd, 2nd ed., 1970.

Cushenberry, Donald C. *Remedial Reading in the Secondary School*. West Nyack, N.Y., Parker Publishing Company Inc., 1972.

Daniels, J. & Diack, H. *The Standard Reading Tests,* London, Chatto & Windus (Educational) Ltd, 1964.

Dechant, E. *Improving the Teaching of Reading*. New Jersey, Prentice-Hall, 1970.

Della-Piana, G. *Reading Diagnosis and Prescription: An Introduction*. New York, Holt, Rinehart & Winston, Inc., 1968.

Diack, H. *Reading and the Psychology of Perception*. New York, Ray Palmer, 1961.

Diack, H. *In Spite of the Alphabet*. London, Chatto & Windus, 1965.

Drummond, D. & Wignell, E. (eds) *Reading: A Source Book for Teachers*. London, Heinemann Educational Books Ltd, 1979.

Duffy, G. & Sherman, G. *Systematic Reading Instruction*. London, Harper & Row, 1972.

Durrell, Donald D. *Improving Reading Instruction*. Tarrytown-on-Hudson, World Book Co., 1956.

Edwards, Peter. 'A Computer Generated Corpus and Lexical Analysis of English Language Instructional Materials Prescribed for Use in British Columbia Junior Secondary Grades'. Unpublished Doctoral Dissertation, University of British Columbia, 1974.

Farr, Roger. *Reading: What Can Be Measured?* Newark, Delaware, International Reading Association, 1969.

Frierson, E. & Barbe, W. *Educating Children with Learning Disabilities*. New York, Appleton-Century-Crofts, 1967(a).

Fries, C. *Linguistics and Reading*. New York, Holt, Rinehart & Winston, Inc., 1963.

Frostig, M. and Maslow, P. *Learning Problems in the Classroom: Prevention and Remediation*. New York, Grune & Stratton, 1973.

Gagne, R. *Conditions of Learning*. New York, Holt, Rinehart & Winston, Inc., 1965.

Gates, A. *The Improvement of Reading*. New York, The Macmillan Company, 1947.

Gattegno, C. *Words in Colour Teaching Guide*. England, Educational Explorers Ltd, 1962.

Gearhart, B. *Learning Disabilities: Educational Strategies*. St. Louis, The C. V. Mosby Company, 1973.

Gillespie, P.H. and Johnson, L. *Teaching Reading to the Mildly Retarded Child*. Columbus, Ohio, Charles E. Merrill Publishing Co., 1974.

Gilliland, John & Merritt, John. *Readability*. London, University of London Press Ltd, 1972.

Gilliland, Hap. *A Practical Guide to Remedial Reading*. Columbus, Ohio, Charles E. Merrill Publishing Co., 1974.

Goodman, K. *The Psycholinguistic Nature of the Reading Process*. Detroit, Wayne State University Press, 1973.

Gunderson, D. *Language and Reading: An Interdisciplinary Approach*. Centre for Applied Linguistics, 1974.

Guszac, F.J. *Diagnostic Reading Instruction in the Elementary School*. New York, Harper & Row, 1972.

Harris, Albert J. *How to Increase Reading Ability*. New York, David McKay Co. Inc., 1965.

Heilman, Arthur, W. *Principles and Practices of Teaching Reading* Columbus, Ohio, Charles E. Merrill Publishing Co., 3rd ed., 1972.

Huey, E. *The Psychology and Pedagogy of Reading*, London, The M.I.T. Press, 1968.

Ingram, T. *The Nature of Dyslexia*. Bulletin of the Orton Society, Vol. 19, no.18, 1969.

Jackson, M. *Reading Disability: Experiment, Innovation and Individual Therapy*. Angus & Robertson, 1972.

Jones, J.K. *Colour Story Reading Scheme*. London, Nelson, 1967.

Jongsma, Eugene. *The Cloze Procedure as a Teaching Technique*. Newark, Delaware, International Reading Association, 1971.

Keeney, A. & Keeney, V. *Dyslexia: Diagnosis and Treatment of Reading Disorders*. St Louis, The C.V. Mosby Company, 1968.

Kirk, S. *The Diagnosis and Remediation of Psycholinguistic Disabilities*. Part 1. University of Illinois, Institute for Research on Exceptional Children, 1966.

Kottmeyer, William. *Teacher's Guide for Remedial Reading*. St. Louis Webster Publishing Co., 1959.

Money, J. (ed.) *Reading Disability*. Baltimore, The Johns Hopkins Press, 1962.

Money, J. *The Disabled Reader: Education of the Dyslexic Child*. The Johns Hopkins Press, 1967.

Myers, P.I. & Hammill, D.D. *Methods for Learning Disorders*. New York, John Wiley & Sons, Inc., 1976 (revised).

Neisser, U. *Cognitive Psychology*. New York, Appleton-Century-Crofts, 1966.

Nicholson, T. *An Anatomy of Reading*. The Research and Planning Branch, Education Department of South Australia, 1973.

Otto, Wayne & McMenemy, Richard A. *Corrective and Remedial Teaching*. Boston, Houghton Mifflin Co., 1966.

Passow, A. et al. *Education of the Disadvantaged: A Book of Readings*. New York, Holt, Rinehart & Winston, 1968.

Reid, J. (ed.) *Reading: Problems and Practices*. Ward Lock Educational, 1972.

Robinson, H.A. *Meeting Individual Differences in Reading*. Chicago, University of Chicago Press, 1965.

Robinson, H.A. *Reading: Seventy-Five Years of Progress*. Vol.28, The University of Chicago Press, 1967.

Robinson, H.M. *Innovation and Change in Reading Instruction*. Part II. Chicago, The University of Chicago Press, 1968.

Ross, Alan O. *Psychological Aspects of Learning Disabilities and Reading Disorders*. New York, McGraw-Hill Book Company, 1976.

Ruddell, Robert B. *Reading — Language Instruction: Innovative Practices*. Englewood Cliffs, New Jersey, Prentice-Hall, Inc., 1974.

Russell, David H. *Children Learn to Read*. Boston, Ginn and Co, 1961.

Schell, L.M. & Burns, P.C. *Remedial Reading: Classroom and Clinic*. Boston, Allyn & Bacon, Inc., 1972.

Schonell, F. *Backwardness in the Basic Subjects*. London, Oliver & Boyd, 1965.

Schonell, F. *The Psychology and Teaching of Reading*, London, Oliver & Boyd, 5th ed., 1974.

Singer H. & Ruddell, R.B. (eds.) *Theoretical Models and Processes of Reading*. Newark, Delaware, International Reading Association, 1970.

Smith, Frank. *Understanding Reading: Psycholinguistic Analysis of Reading and Learning to Read.* New York, Holt, Rinehart & Winston, Inc., 1971.

Smith, Frank. *Psycholinguistics and Reading.* New York, Holt, Rinehart & Winston, Inc., 1973.

Southgate, V. & Roberts, G. *Reading — Which Approach?* University of London Press, 1970.

Stott, D.H. *Programmed Reading Kit.* Edinburgh, Holmes McDougall Ltd., 1971 (revised).

Tarnopol, L. *Learning Disabilities.* Springfield, Charles C. Thomas, 1971.

Thomas, L.E. & Robinson, A.H. *Improving Reading In Every Class.* Boston, Allyn & Bacon, Inc., 1972.

Thompson, L. *Reading Disability: Developmental Dyslexia.* Springfield, Charles C. Thomas, 1969.

Tinker, Miles A. & McCullough, Constance M. *Teaching Elementary Reading.* New York, Appleton-Century-Crofts, 1968.

Vernon, M. *Reading and Its Difficulties.* Cambridge University Press, 1971.

Wallace, G. and McLoughlin, J.A. *Learning Disabilities: Concepts and Characteristics.* Columbus, Ohio, Charles E. Merrill Publishing Company, 1975.

Wilson, Robert M. *Diagnostic and Remedial Reading.* Columbus, Ohio, Charles E. Merrill Books, Inc., 1967.

Zintz, Miles. *Corrective Reading.* Dubuque, Iowa, William C. Brown Co. Publishers, 1966.

Tests

Durrell Analysis of Reading Difficulty. Harcourt, Brace and World, Inc. (NFER act as agents).

Gates-McKillop Reading Diagnostic Tests. Teachers College Press, New York.

Edwards Reading Test. Heinemann Educational Books Ltd.

For further information on tests and testing see:

Pumfrey, Peter D. *Reading: Tests and Assessment Techniques.* Hodder & Stoughton, 1976.

Journals

Reading (UKRA)
Journal of Research in Reading (UKRA)
Remedial Education (NARE)
Forwards Trends
Education 3-13
Journal of Reading (IRA)
The Reading Teacher (IRA)

Microfilm and Microfiche

A vast amount of relevant information is available from the Educational Resources Information Centre (ERIC) which supplies Copies of documents on microfilm and microfiche from the USA. The two main ERIC reference publications are:

Research in Education (RIE), and

Current Index to Journals in Education (CIJE).

Enquiries should be made through the nearest library facility.

Index

An asterisk indicates the name of a publisher